———————VOLUME ONE———————

PIECING TOGETHER BIBLE PROPHECY

THE RUBIK'S CUBE OF BIBLE PROPHECY

DON WALTON

WESTBOW
PRESS
A DIVISION OF THOMAS NELSON

WestBow Press books may be ordered through booksellers or by contacting:

WestBow Press
A Division of Thomas Nelson
1663 Liberty Drive
Bloomington, IN 47403
www.westbowpress.com
1-(866) 928-1240

Because of the dynamic nature of the Internet, any web addresses or
links contained in this book may have changed since publication and
may no longer be valid. The views expressed in this work are solely those
of the author and do not necessarily reflect the views of the publisher,
and the publisher hereby disclaims any responsibility for them.

Any people depicted in stock imagery provided by Thinkstock are models,
and such images are being used for illustrative purposes only.

Certain stock imagery © Thinkstock.

Scripture taken from the King James Version.

ISBN: 978-1-4497-4353-6 (sc)
ISBN: 978-1-4497-4354-3 (hc)
ISBN: 978-1-4497-4352-9 (e)

Library of Congress Control Number: 2012904835

Printed in the United States of America

WestBow Press rev. date: 05/07/2012

Time For Truth Ministries is a nonprofit ministry dedicated to the purpose of educating today's church about end-time lies and equipping it to combat them with the truths of God's Word. To learn more, visit us on the World Wide Web at www. timefortruth.org

Press Worthy

Contents

The Rubik's Cube of Bible Prophecy

Did you know there is an annual Rubik's Cube world championship? The popular mechanical puzzle, invented in 1974 by an engineer named Erno Rubik, has sold more than 300 million units. At the 2010 world championship, 263 competitors from thirty-three countries competed at working the three-by-three cube in world record time, which is currently 9.86 seconds. Competitors also raced to be the fastest at working the cube blindfolded, with only one hand, and even with their feet.

Although Mr. Rubik's famous cube is a difficult puzzle to work, Bible prophecy is a far more demanding puzzle. Indeed, the puzzle of Bible prophecy is yet to be worked by any man, in spite of the fact that some of history's most brilliant minds have devoted themselves to it. For instance, many people are unaware that Sir Isaac Newton, who many consider to be the father of modern science, actually invented calculus to perform computations he hoped to use to solve the puzzle of Bible prophecy.

I once believed Bible prophecy was like a jigsaw puzzle; if you got it right, every piece would fall perfectly into place. No piece would have to be forced or pushed into place; no piece would have to be trimmed to fit. Instead, every piece would fall effortlessly, naturally, and perfectly into place. When it did, you would know that you had it; that is, you would know that God had given it to you (John 3:27).

Through the years, my problem with the major schools of eschatology—the study of end-times or last things—is that none of them have all the pieces to the prophetic puzzle in place. All of them are guilty of pushing some pieces in place and trimming others to make them fit. Although each school may have some of the pieces, none of them have worked the prophetic puzzle.

None of today's major schools of eschatology have all the pieces to the prophetic puzzle in place. All of them are guilty of pushing some pieces in place and trimming others to make them fit. Although each school may have some of the pieces, none of them have worked the prophetic puzzle.

Despite this, many proponents of today's major schools of eschatology promote their eschatological views as a true test of orthodoxy. They view any disagreement with those views as tantamount to denying the truth of Scripture. Apparently, it has never dawned on these eschatological masterminds that it is possible to disagree with their interpretations of apocalyptic texts without denying the truth of the texts themselves.

Although I once believed Bible prophecy was like a jigsaw puzzle, I now believe it's more like a Rubik's Cube. Whereas jigsaw puzzles may be worked from start to finish without requiring you to undo what you have already worked out, a Rubik's Cube demands that you be willing to undo what you've already done in order to work it. It's this undoing of what we've already worked out—at least what we think we've worked out—that prevents so many from being more successful in solving the prophetic puzzle. Too many Christians today refuse to rethink anything they've painstakingly hammered out on the anvil of personal study. Therefore, whatever they've hammered out is permanently hammered into them, even if it happens to be wrong.

I'm old enough to remember when the Rubik's Cube first came out. Some of my smart-alecky friends would take the puzzle into another room and shortly thereafter emerge with it worked. According to them, the reason they insisted on working the puzzle in private was to keep the secret to solving it concealed from the rest of us. We later learned, however, the real reason why they never worked the puzzle in public. It was to fool us into believing they had worked the puzzle, when, in actuality, they had secretly peeled the colored stickers off so as to stick all of the same-colored ones on the same side.

Many who claim to have worked the prophetic puzzle remind me of my old smart-alecky friends. Rather than work the prophetic puzzle, they actually peel Scripture off the sacred page and out of its context so as to stick it wherever it needs to go to corroborate their end-time hypothesis. Instead of changing their eschatology to fit the Scripture, they change the Scripture to fit their eschatology.

My smart-alecky friends were finally found out when someone carefully examined their handiwork. On careful examination, it was apparent that the colored stickers had been peeled off and reapplied where they did not belong.

When it comes to today's major schools of eschatology, each should be carefully examined. On close examination, it will become evident to all open-minded examiners that some scriptural texts have been peeled out of their context and misapplied to shore up some supposed end-time scenario.

While we should never give up on working the puzzle of Bible prophecy, we should stop using our current suppositions as standards of Christian orthodoxy. Furthermore, we should all acknowledge that none of us have solved the puzzle; therefore, we must be ever ready to redo what we have supposedly already worked out. Otherwise, we'll never be able to solve the Rubik's Cube of Bible prophecy.

Why We Should Study Bible Prophecy

Prophecy is history prewritten. It is the heralding of what will happen before it happens. The biblical prophets were both forthtellers and foretellers. First, they were forthtellers. They spoke forth, or preached, God's Word to the people of their day and time. Second, they were foretellers. They foretold, or predicted, the future for those who would live in subsequent days and times. It is safe to say, therefore, that the biblical prophet possessed both insight and foresight.

According to Deuteronomy 18:20-22, the true test of a prophet was whether his predictions came true. If they did, he was a true prophet of God. He served as God's mouthpiece, a spokesman for God, whose mouth the Spirit had filled with the very words of God. If his predictions did not come true, however, he was a false prophet, a charlatan, who was to be put to death by the people of God for presuming to put words into the mouth of God.

Don Walton

The Apostle Peter explained how the prophets of old spoke only those words the Holy Spirit breathed into them (2 Peter 1:21). It wasn't their opinions they preached but the oracles of God (1 Peter 4:11). Consequently, they were required, under penalty of death, to be 100 percent accurate in all of their prophesying.

Neither Nostradamus, whose vague and pliable prognostications lend themselves to multiple interpretations, nor modern-day prognosticators, who are often wrong but never in doubt, would have fared well or lasted long in ancient Israel. It is doubtful that the likes of Jean Dixon or Edgar Cayce, whose prolific predictions proved on the whole to be about as precise as a dart-throwing monkey's, would have survived a single day in biblical times without being stoned to death.

It has been estimated that two-thirds of the Bible is prophetic either in type, symbol, or direct statement. Interestingly, none of the so-called holy books and sacred writings of the world's other religions contain a single line of prophecy.

Unlike today, it was a serious thing in biblical times to profess to be a prophet of God. Making such a claim meant imperiling your life every time you uttered a prophetic word. There was no margin for error. One mistake and your prophetic career came to an abrupt end.

It has been estimated that two-thirds of the Bible is prophetic either in type, symbol, or direct statement. Interestingly, none of the so-called holy books and sacred writings of the world's other religions contain a single line of prophecy. How do we explain this abundance of prophecy in the Holy Bible and absence of it from all other "holy" books?

I believe the answer to that question is obvious. If the uninspired (at least divinely uninspired) authors of the world's other holy books had attempted to predict the future, their predictions would have proved untrue. As a result, they would have been exposed as frauds, their writings as fictitious, and their teachings as false. To have any hope of perpetrating their religious ruse on the masses, these false prophets had to steer clear of prophecy, abdicating its lofty sphere to God's true seers.

The Bible teaches that only God can predict the future. In Isaiah 46:8-10, the Lord declares, "Remember this . . . I am God, and there is no other; I am God, and there is none like me. Declaring the end from the beginning, and from ancient times the things that are not yet done." Since it is by His divine providence that the future unfolds, it is God alone who can foretell the future (Isaiah 44:6-7).

How about the gods of the world's other religions? According to the Bible, they have all been proven false by their powerlessness to predetermine and their inability to predict future events (Isaiah 41:21-23; 45:20-22). To worship them—nonexistent entities invented in the imaginative minds of men—rather than the one and only true God, who alone determines and declares what the future holds, is the height of folly.

Don Walton

Not only is the God of the Bible shown to be the one and only true God by the fact He alone predicts the future, the Bible is proven to be the Word of God by the fact it alone contains prophecy. Prophecy's peculiarity to the Bible proves the Holy Bible is the world's only holy book. All other so-called holy books are exposed as unholy frauds by the absence of prophecy from their pages.

Why do critics of the Christian faith always concentrate their efforts on trying to destroy the credibility of the Bible, in particularly, the credibility of the Bible's prophetic texts? Is it not because prophecy attests to the Bible's utter reliability and absolute truthfulness? Think about it. Christianity's critics may attempt to explain away: (1) Israel's miraculous crossing of the Red Sea as a mere wading through the shallow waters of the Reed Sea, (2) the manna in the wilderness as a common sap that oozed from a desert plant, (3) the fire that fell on Elijah's Mount Carmel sacrifice as a chance bolt of lightning, (4) the resurrection of our Lord as nothing more than the hallucinations of His disciples, and (5) the Apostle Paul's miraculous conversion on Damascus Road as a sunstroke. Nevertheless, if the Bible predicts the future and its predictions come true, the critics of Christianity are silenced. They are left with nothing to say.

Prophecy's peculiarity to the Bible proves the Holy Bible is the world's only holy book. All other so-called holy books are exposed as unholy frauds by the absence of prophecy from their pages.

Many people argue that we shouldn't bother with the study of prophecy. They insist that it's too difficult to understand. How can anyone see to the bottom of it, they ask, when its waters have been so muddied by so many competing theories? Besides, we don't have to be prophecy wonks to live committed Christian lives, so why even bother with the study of prophecy?

As we have already pointed out, two-thirds of the Bible is prophecy either in type, symbol, or direct statement. Furthermore, about one-fourth of the Bible is predictive prophecy that remains to be fulfilled. In light of this, one cannot help but question the wisdom of advocating the snubbing of so wide a swath of Holy Writ. Moreover, it's hard to see how we can obey the Scriptural admonition—"Study to show [yourselves] approved unto God, [workmen] that needeth not to be ashamed, rightly dividing the word of truth" (2 Timothy 2:15)—if we refuse to study at least a fourth of the Bible.

In my denomination (Southern Baptist), we have always prided ourselves on being a people of the Book. If we are to neglect the study of predictive prophecy, however, we'll have to start calling ourselves a people of three-fourths of the Book. Along with necessitating the modification of our beloved Baptist motto, ignoring prophecy will also result in our forfeiture of a guaranteed blessing. The Bible promises a blessing to everyone who reads and hears its prophetic texts (Revelation 1:3). Although a blessing awaits all who study the Scripture, the only study within Scripture that guarantees us a blessing is the study of prophecy.

Unfortunately, it's not just people in our pews who argue against the study of prophecy but also pastors in our pulpits. Some pastors claim to have given up on the study of prophecy in order to focus on evangelism. They maintain that they would rather win the lost than arguments on eschatology. While this sounds pious, noble, and good, it is fatally flawed in at least three ways.

First, the true minister of God is one who declares the whole Word of God. In Acts 20:27, the Apostle Paul declared himself to be a proven minister of God by the fact that he never hesitated to proclaim to others "the whole counsel of God." The true minister of God does not pick and choose what parts of the Bible to preach and teach. Instead, he preaches the whole Bible, from Genesis to Revelation. Any pastor who refuses to preach and teach on prophecy is withholding from his congregation a great deal of the divine counsel. How, then, can such a pastor be a true minister of God?

Second, in His parable of the faithful and wise servant (Matthew 24:45-51), our Lord explains how those put in charge of the Master's house have the responsibility of feeding His household "meat in due season." This parable is an obvious reference to the responsibility of pastors (those put in charge of the Master's house) to preach and teach to the church (the Master's household) those portions of Scripture (meat in due season) that are most relevant to the day and time within which the church finds itself. It is only by faithfully discharging this trust that pastors enable their congregations to become like "the sons of Issachar"—men and women who have "understanding of the times" and know what they "ought to do" (1 Chronicles 12:32).

The following quote, which is attributed to the great Protestant Reformer Martin Luther, may very well have been penned, whether by him or someone else, with our Lord's parable of the faithful and wise servant in mind: "If I profess with the loudest voice and clearest expression every portion of the truth of God except precisely that little point which the world and the devil are at that moment attacking, I am not confessing Christ, however boldly I may be professing Christ. Where the battle rages, there the loyalty of the soldier is proved, and to be steady on all the battlefield besides is mere flight and disgrace if he flinches at that point."

Along with proving themselves derelict in their divinely appointed duties and keeping their congregations ignorant of the times within which they live, pastors who flinch at preaching and teaching those prophetic portions of Scripture most pertinent to their day are disgracefully disloyal to Christ.

The Bible teaches that "the testimony of Jesus is the spirit of prophecy" (Revelation 19:10). The purpose of prophecy is to testify of Jesus so that men might believe in Him.

Finally, the Bible teaches that "the testimony of Jesus is the spirit of prophecy" (Revelation 19:10). The purpose of prophecy is to testify of Jesus so that men might believe in Him. When a couple of His disciples kept stumbling over their doubts on the road to Emmaus, our Lord helped them hop the hurdles of unbelief by explaining how He personally fulfilled what the prophets had predicted (Luke 24:25-27). A little later, in the same chapter, our Lord does the same thing for the rest of His disciples (Luke 24:44-46). He helps them put their doubts to bed once and for all by showing them in the Scriptures how He personally fulfilled all that was "written in the law of Moses, and in the prophets, and in the psalms, concerning Him."

Notice, it was prophecy that finally led Jesus' disciples to a fixed and firm faith in Him. This explains Jesus' words in John 14:29, "And now I have told you before it come to pass, that, when it is come to pass, you might believe." Truly, the purpose of prophecy, especially fulfilled prophecy, is to produce faith in Christ.

The Apostle Peter says an extraordinary thing in 2 Peter 1:19. He claims that the testimony of eyewitnesses like him is not the most persuasive evidence that the Christian has in presenting his case for Christ to a lost and dying world. Instead, Peter says that our best evidence and most persuasive argument is "the more sure word [testimony] of prophecy." Nothing, according to Peter, is more powerful in persuading men to place their faith in Christ than prophecy.

Any pastor who claims to be ignoring the study of prophecy in order to devote himself to evangelism is foolishly disarming himself of the most powerful weapon he could ever wield in the battle for men's souls. It is therefore the serious student of prophecy, not the neglecter of it, who is most devoted and best equipped to "go forth . . . bearing [the] precious seed" of the gospel and to return "rejoicing bringing [with him] sheaves" of souls for God's eternal garner (Psalm 126:6).

It is truly inconceivable to me how any Christian could advocate the abandonment of a study of Scripture that proves the Bible to be the divinely inspired Word of God, proves the God of the Bible to be the one and only true God, and proves Jesus Christ to be the one and only Savior of the world. If you ask me, few studies, if any, are more important and profitable to the serious student of God's Word than the study of prophecy.

Any pastor who claims to be ignoring the study of prophecy in order to devote himself to evangelism is foolishly disarming himself of the most powerful weapon he could ever wield in the battle for men's souls.

Coming to Terms

To understand Bible prophecy, one must understand the biblical terms employed in its exposition as well as those bantered about in the modern-day debate on this vital subject. What do all of these terms mean? What different meanings are ascribed to them by different schools of thought? And to whom do they mean what?

Prophecy may be defined as prewritten history passed down to us by the biblical prophets who spoke forth the Word of God under the divine inspiration of the Holy Spirit (2 Peter 1:21).

When I was a teenager, an uncle of mine frequently called upon me whenever he needed help digging a footer for an addition to one of his rental houses. I always dreaded to hear his voice on the phone: "Donnie, I need you to come help me dig." Of all the jobs I've ever done, I believe I hate digging the most. Yet, I learned from working with my uncle that you can't build anything unless you dig first.

We all get excited about new houses and buildings. Who doesn't appreciate an architectural masterpiece like India's Taj Mahal?

Still, when it comes to shovels and digging, no one gets excited. We all prefer to keep our hands unsoiled and dirt out from under our fingernails. But without some sweat on someone's brow and a shovel in someone's hand, there would be no houses, buildings, or Taj Mahal.

To build a study of prophecy, we must begin by digging. In this chapter, we'll roll up our sleeves and get our hands dirty. It is only by doing this dirty work first that we will be able to lay a solid foundation for all that follows. Each term discussed in this chapter will serve as a block in the bedrock of what we hope will eventually prove to be a scripturally sound understanding of prophecy.

Prophecy

Obviously, the first term one needs to define in a study of prophecy is the term *prophecy* itself. As we have already noted, prophecy may be defined as history prewritten. The word *prophecy* literally means "to speak forth." The biblical prophets were both forth-tellers and foretellers. They were forth-tellers in that they spoke forth God's message to the people of their own day. They were foretellers in that they also predicted the future for those who would live in latter days. Prophecy may therefore be defined as prewritten history passed down to us by the biblical prophets who spoke forth the Word of God under the divine inspiration of the Holy Spirit (2 Peter 1:21).

15

Dual Prophecy

While you may not be familiar with the term *dual prophecy*, a proper understanding of it is imperative to all who take up the study of prophecy. Any ignorance over this important term will prove to be a serious impediment to any investigation of Bible prophecy.

A dual prophecy is a prophecy that has both an imminent and an ultimate fulfillment. At the time it was prophesied by a biblical prophet, it had an imminent fulfillment in the near future. At the same time, however, it had an additional and ultimate fulfillment in the distant future. Whereas the imminent fulfillment of a dual prophecy may have been literal and physical, the ultimate fulfillment of a dual prophecy may prove to be symbolic and spiritual.

In order to illustrate a dual prophecy, I propose that we set sail from the dock for a short excursion into the study of prophecy itself. Now, we're not going to be gone very long; in fact, we'll be right back, since we've much preparatory work to do before attempting to navigate the vast sea of scriptural prophecy. Still, this quick excursion will illustrate a couple of important things. It will provide you with an excellent example of a dual prophecy as well as illustrate the difficulties with which the study of prophecy is fraught.

An Example of a Dual Prophecy

Although tradition suggests that Joel was one of the earliest prophets of Judah, possibly prophesying during the reign of Joash (830 BC) or the reign of Uzziah (750 BC), the date of his prophecy is uncertain. Suggested dates for the book range widely from a time shortly after 836 BC to an untenable time subsequent to the Babylonian Captivity, sometime around 500 BC.

Since we're unsure of the actual date of Joel's prophecy, we're unsure of when his predicted plague of locusts took place. Some have suggested that it was actually occurring while Joel prophesied, in which case Joel was not predicting what was about to happen but merely describing what was happening (Joel 1:1-12). In any event, the occurring or ominous plague of literal locusts was but a foreshadowing of a far greater judgment soon to befall the people of Judah if they continued to be unrepentant in their rebellion against God (Joel 1:14-15).

Unlike the literal locusts Joel speaks of in chapter one, the locust of Joel 2:1-11 appear to be symbolic, representing an invading enemy army. In the Old Testament, God often used enemy armies as an instrument of judgment against His unrepentant people. If Judah failed to repent and return to God, Joel predicted that a far worse fate than a mere plague of locusts would eventually befall the nation in the coming "day of the Lord" (Joel 2:12-17).

Joel's prophecy of an invading enemy army was partially fulfilled when the Assyrian army, which destroyed the northern kingdom of Israel in 722 BC, invaded the southern kingdom of Judah shortly thereafter. Were it not for King Hezekiah's petitioning of heaven for deliverance from the threatening Assyrian foe and heaven's intervening response, which resulted in the angel of the Lord striking dead 185,000 sleeping Assyrian solders in a single night, Judah, like Israel, would have fallen to the invading Assyrians (see 2 Kings 18-19; 2 Chronicles 32:1-23; Isaiah 36-37).

Despite God's miraculous deliverance of Judah from Assyria, Judah soon forgot about God's intervention on its behalf and forsook Him by returning to its idolatrous ways. As a consequence, the prophecy of Joel was finally fulfilled when the Babylonians invaded Judah and destroyed Jerusalem in 587 BC.

Although one would think that Joel's prophecy had definitely run its course with its initial fulfillment by a literal plague of locusts, its partial fulfillment by the invading Assyrian army, and its final fulfillment by the invading Babylonians, Scripture signals that there yet remains a further future fulfillment of Joel's prophecy in the final "day of the Lord"—God's ultimate judgment upon this Christ-rejecting world. According to Revelation 9:1-11, a passage containing glaring similarities to Joel's ancient prophecy that are anything but coincidental, the consummate fulfillment of Joel's prophecy will not be an invading army of locusts, Assyrians, or Babylonians upon an unrepentant Judah. Instead, it will be an unprecedented demonic invasion upon an unrepentant world.

This multilayered prophecy of the ancient prophet Joel serves as an excellent example of a dual prophecy. It has both imminent and ultimate fulfillments. It is fulfilled literally (locusts), symbolically (Assyrians and Babylonians), and spiritually (demonic entities released from the Abyss who are ruled over by Abaddon). Only by understanding the diverse applications of this dual prophecy can one hope to rightly divide Joel's ancient predictions and arrive at pertinent present-day truths. To mistakenly conclude that Joel's prophecy spoke exclusively of an imminent and literal invasion of locusts upon yesterday's unrepentant Judah would result in us missing the prophecy's true spiritual relevance for us today; namely, its dire warning of an ultimate and unprecedented demonic invasion upon the whole earth at the end of time.

The Day of the Lord

I've always found it interesting that many of the prevalent terms employed by today's prophecy wonks are either not found in the Bible at all or appear only once or twice in all of Scripture. On the other hand, a term like the "day of the Lord," which is strewn throughout the pages of sacred Scripture, is seldom mentioned or penned by prophecy's most popular present-day pundits. One cannot help but ask the question, "Why?" After all, shouldn't the study of prophecy be centered around what the Bible actually says and not around terms that are foreign to Scripture or scarcely found within it? This is not to say that terms concocted and made fashionable by people in their continual commentary on Bible prophecy can never prove to be constructive. It is to say, however, that such man-made terms should never be substituted for or given supremacy over biblical terms themselves, especially those found most frequently in the Scriptures.

When the Bible speaks of "the day of the Lord," as it often does, it is talking about a day of approaching judgment. It is normally speaking of an impending judgment of a particular people at a particular time that points to the ultimate judgment of all people at the end of time. Thus, all "days of the Lord" are a foreshadowing of Christ's climactic and cataclysmic judgment upon the whole earth at His second coming, which will prove to be the consummate "day of the Lord."

Many of the prevalent terms employed by today's prophecy wonks are either not found in the Bible at all or appear only once or twice in all of Scripture. On the other hand, a term like the "day of the Lord," which is strewn throughout the pages of sacred Scripture, is seldom mentioned or penned by prophecy's most popular present-day pundits.

Although every reference in the Bible to the "day of the Lord" is not speaking specifically of Christ's second coming, each reference does serve as a harbinger of it. While a particular reference may be speaking of a past judgment of God on a particular people, it also serves as a foreshadowing of the catastrophic judgment awaiting this Christ-rejecting world when Christ returns to pour out His wrath upon it in great power and glory (Revelation 6:12-17).

Eschatology

Eschatology is just a big word that simply means the study of last things or the end-times. To study prophecy is to study eschatology.

The End-Times

If eschatology is the study of the end-times, then how should we define *the end-times*? To many people today, the end-times are comprised of a short span of time that occurs just before the second coming of Jesus Christ. To them, the end-times are the very last days of the last days. To the authors of the New Testament, however, the end-times commenced with the first advent of Christ (the Incarnation) and will continue until consummated at the second advent of Christ (the Second Coming). Thus, everyone living between the two advents of Christ is living in the end-times, including you and I.

> *The end-times commenced with the first advent of Christ (the Incarnation) and will continue until consummated at the second advent of Christ (the Second Coming).*

The Three Major Interpretive Views of Eschatology

In a later chapter, we will deal with the important issue of whether Bible prophecy should be interpreted literally or figuratively. As we will point out at that time, there is probably no more determinative factor in your understanding of prophecy than whether you interpret it literally or figuratively.

In this section, however, we're not dealing with how to interpret the prophetic Scriptures but with the three major interpretive views of eschatology. Now, there may be a thousand and one different schools of eschatology within these three major interpretive views, but there are only three major interpretive views of eschatology. Rather than get into all of the different schools found within each major interpretive view, which would undoubtedly leave us as confused as drunken cowboys in a cattle stampede, we will limit ourselves at this point to a discussion of the three major interpretive views.

A little later in this chapter, we'll take up and elaborate upon today's three most prominent schools of eschatology. In doing so, we'll avoid like the plague the plethora of other schools, lest this manuscript become thicker than the New York phone directory and you, the reader, drowned in a bottomless sea of endless theories and speculations.

1. Preterist

The first of the three major interpretive views of eschatology is called preterism. The word *preterist* means "past in fulfillment." Preterists are people who interpret Bible prophecy to be past in fulfillment. For instance, the preterist interprets the prophecies of the book of Revelation as having been fulfilled in the early years of the church, a period which culminated in Titus the Roman's destruction of Jerusalem in 70 AD.

Since John the Revelator could not have possibly been predicting what had previously happened, the preterist argues against the traditional dating of the book of Revelation (95/96 AD) and for a much earlier date (68/69 AD). Preterism's viability as a tenable interpretive view of eschatology is therefore wholly dependent upon an earlier dating of the Apostle John's penning of the Apocalypse.

2.   Historicist

The second of the three major interpretive views of eschatology is called historicism. The *historicist* is someone who interprets Bible prophecy as being fulfilled throughout history. Some prophecy has been fulfilled in the past; some is now being fulfilled in the present; and some awaits fulfillment in the future.

3.   Futurist

The final major interpretive view of eschatology is called futurism. The *futurist* is someone who interprets Bible prophecy as awaiting fulfillment in the future. According to the futurist, all prophecies relating to the "last days," such as those found in the books of Daniel and Revelation, will be fulfilled in a short period of time prior to the second coming of Jesus Christ.

Millennium

Since it forms the centerpiece of today's three most prominent schools of eschatology, not to mention the fact that all three also derive their names from it, the term *millennium* is one of major importance to all contemporary students of Bible prophecy. Though the term is placed on the loftiest of pedestals by present-day prophecy pundits, it is a term not found on the pages of sacred Scripture.

The word *millennium* comes from two Latin words. The first, *mille*, means "thousand," and the second, *annus*, means "years." Thus, the word *millennium* literally means "a thousand years" or "a thousand year period."

In eschatology, the word *millennium* refers to Christ's biblically predicted thousand-year reign upon the earth. Although it may come as quite a surprise, this prediction of a specific "thousand year" reign of Christ upon the earth occurs only once in all of Scripture. In this one instance, Revelation 20:1-10, the phrase "thousand years" appears six times in ten verses.

Granted, it may be easily and evidently argued that the Bible is riddled with references to Christ's millennial reign upon the earth. While Revelation 20:1-10 may be the only specific reference to a "thousand years," there are obviously other references within Scripture that become inexplicable if applied to anything other than Christ's millennial reign upon the earth, such as those that speak of paradisiacal conditions on earth (Isaiah 2:1-5; 11:1-10; 35:1-10; 65:17-25), of the kingdom being restored to Israel (Acts 1:6-7; 3:19-21), and of Christians reigning with Christ upon the earth (2 Timothy 2:12; Revelation 5:9-10).

The Three Major Schools of Eschatology

Just as there are three major interpretive views of eschatology, there are also three major schools of eschatology. Now, as we've already alluded, there is a plethora of schools, theories, and speculations on how the biblically predicted end-times will unfold. To attempt a thorough examination of all of these would result in a volume too heavy to lift and in a manuscript being perpetually penned because of the incessant spawning of new schools of thought. It would also result in further confusion over Bible prophecy rather than any clarification of it. Thus, we will carefully keep the lid on this Pandora's Box by restraining ourselves at this point from delving into anything other than today's three most popular schools of eschatology.

1. Amillennialism

The word *amillennial* literally means "no-millennium." However, this title misrepresents both amillennialism and amillennialists, since amillennialists do not believe that there is no millennium. They only believe that the millennium is to be interpreted figuratively or symbolically rather than literally.

An important distinguishing distinctive of amillennialism is its insistence that there is no trenchant differentiation between

Israel and the church. Amillennialists see the promises made to national Israel in the Old Testament as figurative promises to the "New Israel"—the church—in the New Testament.

To the amillennialists, the millennium is actually occurring right now. It is to be figuratively understood as the church age, a time within which the reign of Christ is to be found in the hearts of Christians. The millennium is not to be understood as a literal thousand-year period but as a symbolic period between Christ's first and second advents, a period which will conclude with the second coming of Jesus Christ in power and glory.

According to amillennialists, when Christ returns there will be a general resurrection of the dead and a final judgment of all mankind. All who have received Christ will be assigned to eternal bliss and all who have rejected Him to eternal punishment. Afterward, the earth will be destroyed by fire and new heavens and a new earth will be created within which righteousness alone will dwell.

Although there is much more to amillennialism, this is amillennialism in a nutshell. As a major school of eschatology, I find that it has much to commend it. I believe it does work some of the prophetic puzzle. Yet, its strained interpretations of some prophetic passages simply can't be forced into the prophetic puzzle where amillennialists try to fit them. For this reason, I'm not an amillennialist, despite the fact that I agree with amillennialists on several important points.

2. Postmillennialism

The word *postmillennialism* literally means "after the millennium." Postmillennialism teaches that Christ will come back after the millennium. The postmillennialist believes that the church will actually convert the whole world, Christianize the whole planet, and conquer the whole earth through its faithful and Spirit-anointed preaching of the gospel. By doing so, the church will usher in the millennium, which the postmillennialist defines as a golden age of Christianity. After the millennium, Jesus will come back to a world that is prepared not only for His coming but also for His coronation.

Of the three major schools of eschatology, I believe this one has the least to commend it. Never mind that the world is getting worse and worse rather than better and better and that the church's influence in the world is rapidly diminishing rather than ever-increasing; there is simply nothing in the Scripture that even hints at such an end-time scenario as the one painted by postmillennialists. Still, postmillennialism survives today as a major school of eschatology thanks to the social gospel being promoted by liberals in mainline denominations and by other postmillennial proponents, particularly those found in charismatic circles who have both resuscitated and relabeled postmillennialism as dominionism, reconstructionism, and the "kingdom now movement."

3. Premillennialism

The word *premillennial* literally means "before the millennium." Premillennialism teaches that Christ will return before the millennium and personally inaugurate His millennial kingdom. While there are multiple schools of premillennialism today, some of which are relatively new and highly questionable, the premillennial view of Christ's second coming was undoubtedly the view of the early church. It is also the only modern-day millennial view that dates back to apostolic times.

Although there are many different types of premillennialists, all premillennialists fall into one of two camps. They are either historicists or futurists; none are preterists. The premillennial historicist believes that prophecy, even that pertaining to the last days and end-times, is being fulfilled throughout history. Some prophecy was fulfilled at Christ's first advent. Some is being fulfilled now, between the two advents of Christ. And all will finally be fulfilled at the second advent of Christ.

The premillennial historicist's view of Bible prophecy appears to have been the commonly held view in the early church. It is also the only contemporary view of the second coming of Jesus Christ that is traceable back to the apostolic age. This is of no little significance!

As far as we can tell, the premillennial historicist's view of Bible prophecy appears to have been the commonly held view in the early church. It is also the only contemporary view of the second coming of Jesus Christ that is traceable back to the apostolic age. This is of no little significance! If the commonly held view of Christ's second coming among the divinely inspired authors of the New Testament, their contemporaries, and the church of the first century was premillennial historicism, then this alone lends great credence to this particular view of eschatology.

Unlike the premillennial historicist, the premillennial futurist believes that all prophecy relating to the last days or end-times awaits fulfillment in the future. Premillennial futurists believe prophecy will be fulfilled in a very short span of time just prior to the second coming of Jesus Christ. This futurist view of prophecy is relatively new. In fact, its history can be traced back no further than the first half of the nineteenth century. Before the year 1830, premillennial futurism was literally unknown and unheard of in all the annals of Christian history.

Just as all premillennialists fall into one of two camps—historicists or futurists—all premillennial futurists fall into one of four camps: pretribulationists, midtribulationists, posttribulationists, or pre-wrath tribulationists. In order to understand these terms and their respective camps, we must familiarize ourselves with two other important terms.

The Tribulation

In the vernacular of premillennial futurism, *the tribulation* is a seven-year period of unprecedented tribulation immediately preceding Christ's return to the earth to establish His millennial kingdom. Although the Bible unquestionably speaks of "tribulation" and even of "great tribulation" prior to the second coming of Jesus Christ, nowhere does it specify a seven-year period as "the tribulation" or the last three and a half years of that seven-year period as "the great tribulation."

As any serious student of the Bible knows, the number seven has great significance in Scripture. Therefore, Scripture's failure to specify anywhere on its sacred pages a seven-year period as "the tribulation" should raise serious questions about this major component of premillennial futurists' end-time scenario. Not even the book of Revelation, which is a book of sevens, mentions a seven-year period. It mentions seven spirits (1:4), seven churches (1:11), seven golden candlesticks (1:12), seven stars (1:16), seven seals (5:1), seven horns (5:6), seven eyes (5:6), seven angels (8:2), seven trumpets (8:2), seven thunders (10:3), seven thousand slain (11:13), seven heads (12: 3; 13:1; 17:3), seven crowns (12:3), seven plagues (15:1), seven bowls (15:7), seven mountains (17:9), and even seven kings (17:10). Yet, it never mentions seven years.

In light of this, one cannot help but ask what biblical basis premillennial futurists have for their supposed seven-year tribulation period. The answer is one solitary passage of

Scripture; namely, Daniel's incredible prophecy of the seventy weeks (Daniel 9:24-27). Without this one passage and their peculiar interpretation of it, premillennial futurists have no Scriptural peg to hang their "tribulational" hat on. In the next volume in this series, we will take up this incredible prophecy, refute the premillennial futurists' interpretation of it, and watch as their seven-year "tribulation" falls to the floor of unscriptural supposition.

The Rapture

According to premillennial futurism, the rapture is the secret return of Christ to snatch His church out of the world. The word *rapture* does not appear anywhere in the Bible. It comes from the Latin Vulgate. The Vulgate was a fifth century translation of the Bible into Latin by Jerome. It served as the main Bible of the Latin-speaking medieval Western church until the time of the Reformation.

Then we which are alive and remain shall be caught up together with them in the clouds, to meet the Lord in the air: and so shall we ever be with the Lord. (1 Thessalonians 4:17)

In the Vulgate, the Greek word for "caught up" in 1 Thessalonians 4:17 is translated into the Latin word *rapere*. It is from this Latin word that we get our English word *rapture*.

Whereas all Bible-believing Christians—there is no other kind of Christian than a Bible-believing one—believe in the "catching up" of 1 Thessalonians 4:17, there is much disagreement among Christians as to the timing of this event. All Christians should be able to honestly agree, however, that before the nineteenth century, particularly before the year 1830, all premillennial views of our Lord's return had two things in common.

First, the "catching up" or "rapture" of 1 Thessalonians 4:17 was not held to be distinct from the second coming of Jesus Christ. Instead, it was viewed synonymously with Christ's second coming.

Prior to 1830, every saint saw the second coming as a single event. There was no belief in a two-staged second coming. No one believed that there would first be a secret coming of Christ to snatch His saints out of the world and then a later visible coming of Christ with His saints to judge the world. The contemporary distinctions made between the "Rapture" and the "Revelation" of Christ or between Christ's "Epiphany" and His "Parousia" were absolutely unheard of. No such distinctions had ever been made.

Second, prior to 1830, all premillennialists believed that the second coming of Christ and our being "caught up" to Him in the air would take place after the biblically predicted tribulation of the last days. This biblically predicted tribulation was not understood as a specific seven year period, but simply as a time of unprecedented troubles divinely predestined to befall our world before the end of the age.

1. Pretribulationism

Now that we understand what premillennial futurists believe about "the tribulation" and "the rapture," we can define and explain each of the four camps of premillennial futurism. The first is pretribulationism. The pretribulationist believes that Christ will rapture His church before the seven-year tribulation period begins, sparing His saints from suffering any end-time trouble.

2. Midtribulationism

The second camp of premillennial futurists is midtribulationism. The midtribulationist believes that Christ will rapture His church in the middle of the seven-year tribulation period, sparing His saints from the "Great Tribulation," which is the last three and a half years of the seven years and the most perilous part of the tribulation period.

3. Pre-Wrath Tribulationism

The third camp of premillennial futurists is pre-wrath tribulationism. The pre-wrath tribulationist believes that Christ will rapture His church just before the end of the seven-year tribulation period, sparing the saints from the wrath of God that will be poured out on a Christ-rejecting world. This belief is in accordance with the words of the Apostle Paul in 1 Thessalonians 5:9: "For God hath not appointed us to wrath, but to obtain salvation by our Lord Jesus Christ."

4. Posttribulationism

The fourth and final camp of premillennial futurists is posttribulationism. The posttribulationist believes that Christ will rapture the church after the seven-year tribulation period, not sparing His saints from any of the end-time tribulation.

Dispensationalism

Before concluding this chapter, we need to define two other important terms in the modern-day debate on eschatology. The first is *dispensationalism* and the second is *premillennial dispensationalism*. Both of these terms are associated with today's most popular school of eschatology, a school of premillennial futurists from the pretribulationists' camp that is so popular with evangelicals that many evangelicals now equate it with doctrinal orthodoxy. In other words, any disagreement with this widely accepted school of eschatology is paramount in the minds of many evangelicals to heresy on the part of all dissenters.

Dispensationalism is the belief that history should be divided into separate dispensations or ages. In each dispensation, man is tested by God as to his obedience to God's revealed will for that particular period of time. According to dispensationalism, there are at least seven dispensations:

1. The Age of Innocence—from creation to the fall

2. The Age of Conscience—from the fall to the flood

3. The Age of Government—from Noah to Abraham

4. The Age of Promise or Patriarchs—from Abraham to Moses

5. The Age of Law—from Moses to Jesus

6. The Age of Grace or the Church Age—from the Incarnation to the Second Coming

7. The Kingdom or Millennial Age—the millennial reign of Christ, which commences at Christ's second coming

Adherence to dispensationalism necessitates a "rightly divided" interpretation of God's Word. All Scripture must be exclusively applied to its dispensation alone. In the dispensationalist's mind, some Scripture speaks exclusively to one age, other Scripture speaks exclusively to other ages, and no Scripture speaks to all ages. Thus, what God says to Israel has no application to the church, and what God says to the church has no application to Israel. The twain shall never meet; if they should, dispensationalism would be blown to smithereens.

This Israel/church dichotomy is of paramount importance to dispensationalists, not to mention the most important brick in the foundation of today's most popular school of eschatology—premillennial dispensationalism. To the premillennial dispensationalist, God's plans for Israel (His earthly people) and the church (His heavenly people) are totally different and must be kept separate at all times. In addition, these separate plans can never operate concurrently upon the earth, since an eternal God limits Himself to working in only one dispensation at a time.

It is easy to understand from the above why all classical premillennial dispensationalists are pretribulationists. They believe that God cannot turn back to His plan for Israel until the church is removed from the world, bringing to an end this current dispensation—the church age. Only then can God fulfill His literal promises to the physical descendants of Abraham. If

> To the premillennial dispensationalist, God's plans for Israel (His earthly people) and the church (His heavenly people) are totally different and must be kept separate at all times.

the premillennial dispensationalists cannot keep God's plans for the church and Israel separate from one another at all times, then the rug is pulled out from under their futurist feet and dispensationalism's house of cards comes crashing down.

Premillennial Dispensationalism

Premillennial dispensationalism is undoubtedly the most popular school of eschatology in the world today. Many of today's most popular preachers and Christian authors are premillennial dispensationalists. As stated above, this widely accepted view of the end-times is equated with doctrinal orthodoxy in many evangelical circles. In other words, to disagree with premillennial dispensationalists is to run the risk of being accused of heresy, a potentially ruinous accusation that has a very chilling effect on all honest debate.

Premillennial dispensationalism is the belief that God's new covenant with the church—His heavenly people—is a mere parenthesis or footnote in His ultimate plan to fulfill His old covenant promises to Israel, His chosen and earthly people. This belief exalts Jewry so much in the minds of premillennial dispensationalists that many of them equate any disagreement with them over God's favoring of the Jewish people over all other people as anti-Semitism. In spite of the fact that the Apostle Peter plainly declared in the Gentile home of Cornelius, "Of a truth I perceive that God is no respecter of persons" (Acts 10:34), premillennial dispensationalists insist that God is a respecter of persons, making such a huge distinction between Jews and Gentiles that His plan for the former is primary and for the latter only secondary.

Premillennial dispensationalism is the belief that God's new covenant with the church—His heavenly people—is a mere parenthesis or footnote in His ultimate plan to fulfill His old covenant promises to Israel, His chosen and earthly people.

To illustrate the inordinately high pedestal that premillennial dispensationalists have erected for the exaltation of the Jewish people, permit me to share a couple of quotes from one of their foremost proponents. In a 2006 newsletter, Dave Hunt, a prolific author and popular premillennial dispensationalist apologist, wrote, "Unquestionably, Israel is the major subject of God's Holy Word." I find Hunt's statement to be far from unquestionable; in fact, I find it to be indefensible, especially in light of the fact that Jesus plainly declared Himself to be the major subject of God's Holy Word. In John 5:39, Christ clearly states, "Search the scriptures; for in them ye think ye have eternal life: and they are they which testify of me." The whole purpose of the Scripture is to testify of Christ, so that all people, both Jews and Gentiles, will come to Him.

In Hunt's August 2006 newsletter, he went so far as to suggest that Christ "is coming in power and glory to punish the world for its abuse of His people Israel." I thought Christ was coming back to judge the world for its rejection of Him. Aren't our eternal destinies determined by what we do with Jesus, rather than by how we treat Jewish people? Don't get me wrong, the mistreatment of Jewish people, just like the mistreatment of any people, is an inexcusable crime against God and humanity. Like all forms of racism and fascism, anti-Semitism is equally deplorable. Nevertheless, it is not the reason for God's impending judgment upon our world. It is our world's rejection of Jesus Christ alone that has put us in the crosshairs of divine retribution.

Sometime ago, my administrative assistant shared an email with me from a retired Baptist minister. Although I was unfamiliar with the man, I was able to easily discern that he was a member of the premillennial dispensationalists' camp. In his email, he alleged the "primary reason the United States has been so blessed by God is that it has been a safe haven for God's people, the Jews." He went on to add, "That's about the only thing left that stays God's wrath from coming big time on [our] country." Now, I don't know about you, but to suggest that a nation's treatment of Jewish people, regardless of how it treats other people, is the determining factor in whether it is blessed by God or judged by God is way over the top to me.

No one who believes the Bible can deny that Israel plays a special role in God's plans and purposes. Furthermore, as Paul indicates in Romans 9-11, Israel's role in God's plan is not yet played out. Still, in spite of the undeniable importance of Israel in the plans and purposes of God, there is no justification for the preferential status and inflated importance that premillennial dispensationalists assign to the Jewish people in the divine program.

God has a special plan for your life and mine, but this doesn't mean that he favors you and me over other people. Neither does it mean that our need of Christ is any less than anyone else's or that God sees our standing in Christ as superior to any other Christian's. Likewise, God's special plan for the Jews should not be misinterpreted into some kind of divine discrimination against Gentiles. Neither should we erroneously conclude that

> *God's special plan for the Jews should not be misinterpreted into some kind of divine discrimination against Gentiles.*

Jewish people somehow need Christ less than others or that Jewish Christians are somehow given a superior standing in Christ.

Along with condemning everyone as being anti-Semitic who disagrees with them over God's preferential treatment of the Jews, many premillennial dispensationalists also condemn everyone as being a heretic who refuses to elevate Old Testament shadows over New Testament substance. Despite the fact that the book of Hebrews teaches that the new covenant is a "better covenant" with "better promises" (Hebrews 8:6), premillennial dispensationalists insist that the old covenant with its inferior promises actually takes precedence over the new. In fact, many suggest that God just threw in the church and the new covenant to fill in the gap until the time comes for Him to once again turn His attention back to Israel and the old covenant.

This explains the premillennial dispensationalist's preoccupation with the following:

1. The nation of Israel, instead of the church, which Paul calls "the Israel of God" (Galatians 6:16).

2. The naturally born physical seed of Abraham, instead of the supernaturally born spiritual seed of Abraham (Galatians 3:29).

3. Middle Eastern real estate, instead of a "better" and "heavenly" country (Hebrews 11:16).

4. The earthly city of Jerusalem, instead of the "heavenly Jerusalem," a city "whose builder and maker is God" (Hebrews 11:10, 12:22).

5. A rebuilt Jewish temple, instead of the church, which is the "holy temple" and "spiritual habitation" of God in the world today (Ephesians 2:19-22).

6. Reestablished animal sacrifices, instead of the once and for all sacrifice of Christ upon the cross of Calvary, which has done away with all other sacrifices for sin (Hebrews 10:10, 26).

7. A reinstituted Levitical priesthood comprised of Levites alone, instead of the "royal priesthood" comprised of all believers in Jesus Christ (1 Peter 2:9).

8. The issue of whether Jews or Gentiles are governing Palestine, instead of whether Jews and Gentiles are going to heaven!

As the above clearly illustrates, premillennial dispensationalism does great violence to the progression of Bible prophecy. Instead of going from the shadows of the Old Testament's types-of-Christ to the substance of Christ Himself in the New

Testament, and then from the New Testament substance to the spiritual realities that are ours in Christ today, premillennial dispensationalism teaches that the ultimate fulfillment of Bible prophecy is found in a return to Old Testament types and shadows. Such a hypothesis flies in the face of Scripture and shifts the divine text into reverse. It is tantamount to telling someone with an earned PhD that a repeat of preschool will prove to be his ultimate educational experience.

Other glowing problems with this widely accepted modern-day school of eschatology will be enumerated throughout the balance of this and future volumes. Permit me at this point, however, to conclude this present chapter with a simple timetable of how premillennial dispensationalists paint the playing out of the end-times.

THE TIMES OF THE GENTILES—the church age (Luke 21:24)

THE RAPTURE—the first part of the second coming of Christ (1 Thessalonians 4:17)

THE TRIBULATION—the seventieth week of Daniel (Daniel 9:24-27)

THE ABOMINATION OF DESOLATION—the Antichrist's desecration of a rebuilt Jewish temple (Matthew 24:15; Mark 13:14)

THE GREAT TRIBULATION—the last three and a half years of the seven-year tribulation period (Matthew 24:21)

THE BATTLE OF ARMAGEDDON—the gathering together of the world's forces against God and His anointed. (Revelation 16:16)

THE REVELATION—the second part of the second coming of Christ. (Matthew 24:30; Mark 13:26)

THE BEAST AND THE FALSE PROPHET THROWN INTO THE LAKE OF FIRE (Revelation 19:20)

THE MILLENNIUM—Satan bound. (Revelation 20:1-6)

GOG AND MAGOG—Satan loosed. (Revelation 20:7-9)

SATAN THROWN INTO THE LAKE OF FIRE (Revelation 20:10)

THE GREAT WHITE THRONE JUDGEMENT—the judgment of the lost (Revelation 20:11-15)

THE NEW HEAVENS AND THE NEW EARTH—the eternal state (Revelation 21:1-5)

A Brief History of Modern-Day Eschatology

Many modern-day Christians presume that today's patented eschatological views have been around since the dawn of the Christian Era. Furthermore, many believe that their particular view of eschatology is the same as that of the apostles and early church fathers. Rarely do you run across an honest scholar like the late Dr. John Walvoord, who readily admitted that his premillennial dispensational view of eschatology was unheard of before the nineteenth century.

Most Christians today prefer to avoid looking into the history of modern-day schools of eschatology. Apparently, insecurities over their personal end-time beliefs render any study of the history of modern-day schools of eschatology too uncomfortable for them to conduct. While this avoidance of such a vital component to the understanding of modern-day eschatological views leaves them ignorant of how we derived these various schools of thought, it does allow today's Christians to cherry-pick the Scripture and the writings of the early church fathers in an attempt to prove that their personal view of eschatology has been the church's orthodox view all the way back to the first century.

It is important for us to understand that our view of Bible prophecy is neither proved nor disproved by its longevity. This is not to say that the views of the divinely inspired authors of Scripture and their contemporaries are unimportant. Obviously, their views give credence to all similar views today. The problem, however, is found in the fact that we have no detailed spelling-out or systematizing of the eschatological views of Scripture's authors or their contemporaries in any of their writings. Thus, we are left to sparsely glean from their writings what little we can as well as to surmise from these sparse gleanings whatever suppositions we can without any pretense of dogmatism.

Instead of the longevity of our eschatological views, what really proves or disproves them is how well they square with the clear teachings of Scripture. While the Bible may not tell us everything we want to know about prophecy, it does tell us everything we need to know. Whereas it doesn't provide us with enough information to produce haughtiness, it does provide us with enough information to produce hope. Within the needed information provided by the Word of God may be found certain clearly taught prophetic tenets. It is to the degree that our personal beliefs about the end-times line up with these clear biblical tenets that we may determine the validity of our eschatology.

The late J. M. Carroll erroneously concluded that the Baptist church was proven to be the only New Testament church by the fact that Baptists alone can trace their footprints back to New Testament times. Ever since the publishing of Carroll's book, *The Trail of Blood*, Landmark Baptists have insisted that they are not Protestants; rather, they are the present-day inheritors of New Testament Christianity that began with John the Baptist and has continued unabated down through the centuries.

Although J. M. Carroll's romp through history puts Baptists in bed with some pretty strange bedfellows, not to mention heretics, my real fault with his work is the faulty premise upon which it is based. To be a New Testament church does not require tracing one's footprints back to John the Baptist's first baptismal service at the river Jordan. Instead, it only requires a church to be solidly and soundly based upon the teachings of the New Testament.

Likewise, the validity of our understanding of Bible prophecy should be gauged by how scripturally sound it is, not by the fact that we can trace it back to a sermon of the Apostle Paul's. Granted, our understanding of Bible prophecy should never be in contradiction with the Pauline Epistles, but it doesn't have to be traced back to three points and a poem first preached by Paul in the city of Philippi and then handed down through succeeding generations to the adherents of our particular present-day school of eschatology. Don't get me wrong; it would be nice if we could do this, but unfortunately, we can't.

We simply lack the historical wherewithal to build such airtight cases for our present-day end-time beliefs.

Just as Landmark Baptists consider anyone scrutinizing Carroll's version of Baptist history a heretic, many today see any scrutiny of the history of their particular brand of eschatology as heresy. This fact was recently brought home to me in a most undeniable way. On a recent Sunday evening, I taught a lesson in my church on the history of today's most popular school of eschatology. I merely told the history of its development by presenting to my congregation the facts, figures, and dates. Afterward, I was told that some visitors to our evening service left the church irate, feeling that I had poked fun at their personal beliefs. Needless to say, I was dumbfounded, especially in light of the fact that I personally share some of their end-time beliefs.

Upon further query and contemplation, I came to the conclusion that what really irritated these folks was the discovery that their particular brand of eschatology had been fleshed out over time, instead of dropped out of heaven into their predecessors' laps and passed down from one generation to the next untainted. Any serious study of Christian history, whether it is the history of the English Bible or that of modern-day schools of eschatology, will lead the honest student around many unexpected turns and down into some deep dark valleys, where both shining saints and unscrupulous scoundrels will be encountered. Still, this fleshing out of divine providence in the preservation of both God's Word and its eternal truths should not cause us undue consternation; after all, what other feet are available for God's use in the running of His Word and its truths down through the ages than man's frail feet of clay?

The imperfections of God's witnesses can do nothing to take away from the perfection of God's Word. Apparently, many Christians today are like the rich man who lifted up his eyes in torment; that is, they believe that the Word of God—"Moses and the prophets"—is insufficient to lead their "brethren" to faith (Luke 16:19-31). They believe that God's Word is only credible when carried by miraculous rather than mortal messengers. Yet, as Abraham pointed out to the rich man, the Word of God stands on its own merits and is sufficient in and of itself to lead men to faith. It needs not the additional authentication of supernatural heralds or spotless histories. This should not be misinterpreted to mean that it is anything less than crucial for us to practice what we preach. Instead, it should only be understood to mean that the imperfections of God's witnesses can do nothing to take away from the perfection of God's Word.

Far from causing us great distress, the fact that the eschatological truths of the Bible are being figured out over time and are becoming clearer to us as we approach the end of time should be acknowledged as a truth that is actually hinted at in Scripture. For instance, in Genesis 5:21 we are told that Enoch's son was named "Methuselah." According to Genesis 5:27, Methuselah lived to the ripe old age of 969, which makes him the oldest man in the Bible. It is not Methuselah's longevity, however, but his unusual moniker that serves our purposes at this point.

The Hebrew name "Methuselah" actually means "when he dies it shall come." A quick computation of biblical dates will reveal that the flood came the same year Methuselah died. Granted, Methuselah's cryptic moniker failed to specify what was coming and when it would come. It only pointed to the fact that whatever it was would happen when Methuselah died.

Although this first prophecy of the coming flood was nonspecific, later prophesies were very specific, even to the point of pinpointing the flood's starting point. Take, for example, Genesis 6:3, where God specifically warned the prediluvian world that it had but 120 more years to repent. Even more specific is Genesis 7:4, where God precisely pinpointed for Noah that in seven days it would begin to rain for forty days and forty nights. Notice that as the flood drew closer the prophecies concerning it became clearer and clearer.

How many times do we read in the New Testament that the disciples failed to understand prophecy until after Jesus fulfilled it? Time and time again we are told that it was not clear to Christ's disciples until He pointed them back to it in His explanation of it or until they looked back upon it themselves through the eyes of the Spirit with 20/20 hindsight (Mark 9:31-32; Luke 9:43-45; 18:31-34; 24:1-8, 25-27, 44-48; John

2:18-22; 12:12-16; 14:25-26; 16:4). Likewise, much of the Bible's unfulfilled prophecy may remain unclear to Christ's present-day disciples until we approach the time of its fulfillment. Only when all of the pieces begin falling into place will we be able to see the whole prophetic puzzle clearly.

In Matthew 24:33-34, Jesus explains how the generation that sees all the predicted signs of the times fulfilled will not pass away until all of prophecy is fulfilled. The closer we get to the end, the more signs of the times will appear, and the easier it will be for us to read the signs and know with an ever-increasing certainty that the coming of Christ is imminent. It's like going on a long trip. When you first start out, there are no signs along the road telling you about your destination. As you get closer, however, signs about your destination begin to appear. Finally, once you arrive, all the signs are about your destination.

As soon as all the signs of the times appear, we'll know that we've arrived at the end of time. Furthermore, we'll be able to better interpret the signs *Each succeeding generation should see prophecy clearer than the generation that preceded it.* as we see all the pieces to the prophetic puzzle falling into place before our very eyes. It is this generation that will not only see prophecy fulfilled but will also be far more capable of figuring it out than all previous generations. Still, until then, each succeeding generation should see prophecy clearer than the generation that preceded it.

The Histories of Amillennialism and Postmillennialism

The historical tracks of both amillennialism and postmillennialism lead us back to the same individual, a man named Augustine (354-430 AD). Augustine was the bishop of Hippo, which is the ancient name of present-day Annaba, Algeria. Not only is Augustine numbered among the church fathers—the early and influential theologians and writers of Christianity—but he is also deemed to have had more influence on the development of Western Christianity than any other member of this illustrious band.

Augustine is famous for having framed some of Christianity's most important doctrines, such as the doctrines of original sin and just war. He is also known as "the father of amillennialism." This distinction is due to the fact that he is the first known person to have ever taught that the millennium is not to be understood literally but figuratively as the time between the first and second advents of Christ.

Although Augustine is known as "the father of amillennialism," postmillennialism must also be traced back to Augustine, since prior to him all views of Christ's second coming appear to have been premillennial. This is not to say that Augustine was a postmillennialist; he was definitely an amillennialist. It is to say, however, that without Augustine, postmillennialism would have had no figurative interpretive foundation upon which to be built.

It may be argued that the novel notion of postmillennialism—the church's eventual triumph over the world—had initially surfaced prior to Augustine, during the days of Constantine's "Christianizing" of the Roman Empire, a process which began with Constantine's Edict of Milan in 313 AD. Still, Augustine was never caught up in such wishful euphoria. Instead, he insisted in his classic work, *The City of God*, that Christians focus on the promotion of heaven rather than on earthly politics.

Lacking the optimism necessary to give birth to postmillennialism, Augustine planted the pessimistic seeds that germinated into amillennialism. The birth of postmillennialism would be postponed to a later time, since the embryonic euphoria conceived in the church during the days of Constantine ended up violently aborted by the rise of militant Islam in the seventh century, not to mention the fact that it had already been considerably dimmed by the blackening darkness of the Dark Ages (476-1000 AD).

It was not until the time of the Protestant Reformation that the church finally emerged from the darkness of the Dark Ages. In spite of the fact that God used them to lead the church out of papal bondage and back into "the perfect law of liberty" (the Bible), the Protestant Reformers, like the Catholic Augustine before them, were a pessimistic lot of amillennialists. There was, however, a glaring difference between the amillennialism of the Protestant Reformers and that of Augustine, who predated them by more than a thousand years; namely, the Reformers' firmly held belief that the pope was the Antichrist and that the Roman Catholic Church was "MYSTERY, BABYLON THE GREAT, THE MOTHER OF HARLOTS AND ABOMINATIONS OF THE EARTH" (Revelation 17:5).

Though the Catholic Augustine would have never imagined such a belief in his day, the Protestant Reformers so popularized it in theirs that it is still widespread among today's amillennialists. It is also very popular among present-day premillennialists. That such a belief possesses an unpartisan appeal to both amillennialists and premillennialists may be attributed to its undeniable credence, which is shored up in no small part by the documented dark deeds of the Roman Catholic Church from the days of the Dark Ages to the present.

It was not until the post-Reformation era that postmillennialism actually appeared on the eschatological horizon. Its systematizing and spread is attributed to a liberal, freethinking, English preacher by the name of Daniel Whitby (1638-1726). As an alternative to the negativism of amillennialism (the belief in inevitable decay), the positivism of postmillennialism (the belief in eventual utopia) quickly caught on, becoming the dominant eschatology of Europe. One can hardly blame the Europeans for preferring this new positive belief in a triumphant church and a glorious future to the old pessimistic belief in impending tribulation and a gloomy future. Still, the validity of our eschatological views is not founded upon our personal preferences but upon their scriptural soundness.

It is Jonathan Edwards (1703-1758), the predominant preacher in the first Great Awakening, who is credited with the championing and popularizing of postmillennialism in America. With throngs of sinners being converted to Christianity in America's Great Awakenings, and with Christian societies being spawned everywhere for everything from the abolition of slavery to temperance, it was easy for America's Christians to believe that the millennium—the golden age of Christianity—was at the door. Furthermore, it was easy for Christians to persuade their fellow-countrymen of an impending golden age as well, since optimism over the future was already sweeping the country, thanks to things like revolutionary social reforms and tremendous advancements in science and industry.

As it's forever destined to be in a world at enmity with God, the optimistic bubble of postmillennialism was soon burst. One of the main pins to prick it was the French Revolution, which essentially served as a declaration of all out war on the Christian faith. While America's postmillennialists were imagining heaven on earth in the near future, hell on earth had broken out in faraway France.

Despite the fact that this fallen world dealt postmillennialism one severe blow after another, its optimistic bubble was briefly reinflated following World War I. With the founding of President Woodrow Wilson's League of Nations, the precursor to today's United Nations, and the gullible dubbing of World War I as "the war to end all wars," the world was once again susceptible to the postmillennialists' presumption of a prevailing church presiding over a paradisiacal planet. Unfortunately, this naive notion, which was articulated at the time by the credulous words of British Prime Minister Neville Chamberlain—"peace in our time"—was soon trounced by the goose-stepping troops of Nazi Germany's Third Reich.

Reduced to synonymy with liberalism's social gospel following World War II, the sun appeared to be setting on the day of postmillennialism as a major school of eschatology. Then, surprisingly, it made an unforeseen comeback. Today, it is once again embraced by many optimistic souls under the guises of dominionism, reconstructionism, and the "kingdom now movement," all of which are chiefly found within charismatic circles.

The Histories of Premillennialism and Premillennial Dispensationalism

As we've previously pointed out, premillennialists are divided into two camps. There are futurists, and there are historicists. Within each camp there are differing schools of thought, and within these varying schools of thought there are numerous and divergent sects. To trace all of these paths down their particular historical trails would require a historical tracker as competent in research as Daniel Boone was in the wilderness, not to mention a book as bulky as the US tax code. For these reasons, we'll not be taking off down every historical pig trail of premillennialism in this section. Instead, we'll limit ourselves to the history of the two major interpretive views of premillennialism and to the fascinating story behind premillennialism's most popular present-day school of thought.

Premillennial historicism adheres to the belief that Christ will return prior to the millennium and in inauguration of it. It also teaches that Bible prophecy is being fulfilled throughout history; some has been fulfilled in the past, some is being fulfilled in the present, and some will be fulfilled in the future. Of all of the contemporary views of the second coming of Jesus Christ, premillennial historicism appears to be the only one traceable back to the apostolic age. As we've hitherto highlighted, this point is of no little significance. If the commonly held view of Christ's second coming among the divinely inspired authors of the New Testament, their contemporaries, and the church of the first century was premillennial historicism, then this alone lends great credence to this particular interpretive view of eschatology.

Unlike premillennial historicism, the other major premillennial interpretive view of eschatology—premillennial futurism—is not traceable back to the apostolic age. While its belief in Christ's premillennial return to inaugurate His millennial reign squares with that of first century Christians, its insistence upon all "end-time" Bible prophecy awaiting fulfillment in the future is of a much later origin. It is the later origin of this interpretive view that we now take up, believing that by doing so we may shed some needed light upon it.

To begin with, permit me to reiterate the historical fact that it was the dawning of the Protestant Reformation that brought the church out of the long dark night of the Dark Ages. It is nearly impossible to overstate the Protestant Reformation's impact upon our world. It not only aroused Europe from its long slumber of superstition and broke the bonds of a tyrannical papacy, but it gave birth to numerous Protestant nations, which, in turn, gave rise to our modern-day world. Neither the contemporary church, with its emphasis on the priesthood of the believer and congregational church government, nor contemporary society, with its Protestant work ethic, capitalist system, and democratic forms of government, would be in existence today were it not for the paths long blazed before them by the Protestant Reformers.

Although the church emerged from the Dark Ages with its amillennialism intact, it emerged with an addendum to its amillennialism written indelibly on the Protestant psyche with the blood of millions of saints slain during the dark centuries of the Roman Catholic Church's reign of horror. This addendum was the firm belief of the Protestant Reformers that the Antichrist and "MYSTERY, BABYLON THE GREAT, THE MOTHER OF HARLOTS AND ABOMINATIONS OF THE EARTH" were none other than the perpetrators of the Dark Ages' unspeakable crimes against Christianity; namely, the beastly papacy and the whorish Church of Rome. The belief that Catholicism's supposed vicar of Christ (the pope) was actually the Antichrist, contributed in no small way to a mass exodus from Catholicism's congregations and a substantial decrease in its coffers.

To counter the serious blow delivered to it by the Protestant Reformation, the Roman Catholic Church launched a Counter-Reformation. In 1545, the Catholic Church convened its infamous Council of Trent. The purpose of the council was to launch a counterattack against the Protestant Reformers and Protestantism itself. Although convened in 1545, the council continued until 1563, holding eight sessions in Trent (1545-1547) and three sessions in Bologna (1547) under Pope Paul III, five sessions in Trent (1551-1552) under Pope Julius III, and a final nine sessions in Trent (1559-1563) under Pope Pius IV.

Unlike Catholicism's former mode of combating "heretics" and their teachings—the burning of them and their books—a new mode of warfare against Catholic dissenters and papal detractors was called for at Trent; after all, the old way of eliminating all who refused to bow their knees to Rome only added fodder to the fire of Protestant claims that the pope was "the Beast" who "makes war against the saints" (Revelation 13:7). To assist the Catholic Church in its war on Protestantism, the pope recruited the aid of a relatively new order of priests and brothers known as the Society of Jesus. This order, known better today as the

Jesuits, was started in 1534 by a Spanish soldier named Ignatius Loyola.

While recovering from serious wounds received in battle, Ignatius Loyola supposedly underwent a religious conversion and vowed to spend the rest of his life as "a soldier of God." To symbolize the vow he had taken, he placed his weapons on the altar of the monastery of Montserrat, where he alleged to have received a vision of the Virgin Mary and the baby Jesus. Afterward, he recounted a beautiful, reoccurring serpent-like vision that repeatedly consoled him during months of meditation in a cave at nearby Manresa, Catalonia. Upon emerging from the cave at Manresa, Loyola proceeded to devote himself to the study of theology in three of Spain's most prominent universities, the universities of Barcelonia, Alcala, and Salamance. He finally concluded his theological training with an earned masters degree from the College of Montaigu in Paris.

It was while studying in Paris that Loyola and six like-minded followers founded the Society of Jesus, with each declaring their undying allegiance to the pope and taking vows of poverty and chastity. Though the society was initially founded for the purpose of serving as missionaries to the Holy Land, Loyola and his friends eventually ended up in Rome as a sort of secret police for the Vatican. They were given official papal recognition on September 27, 1540, by Pope Paul III, with Ignatius Loyola becoming the society's first superior general or "Black Pope," as the head of the Jesuits is often referred to today.

No order within the Catholic Church has a more nefarious history of intrigue and subterfuge than the Society of Jesus. To separate the factual from the fanciful when it comes to the dark deeds and sinister associates of the Jesuits is no small task. Suffice it to say, for our purposes, that the hands of the Jesuits have been stained throughout their history with the blood of Christian martyrs and clasped from time to time with comrades no less odious than the infamous Illuminati. To prove that this exclamation

"Above all I have learned from the Jesuits. And so did Lenin too, as far as I recall. The world has never known anything quite so splendid as the hierarchical structure of the Catholic Church. There were quite a few things I simply appropriated from the Jesuits for the use of the [Nazi] Party."

is without exaggeration, consider the following words of Adolf Hitler: "Above all I have learned from the Jesuits. And so did Lenin too, as far as I recall. The world has never known anything quite so splendid as the hierarchical structure of the Catholic Church. There were quite a few things I simply appropriated from the Jesuits for the use of the [Nazi] Party."[1]

Along with fighting Protestants over the spoils of men's souls with their customary weaponry of inquisition through torture, the Jesuits were also commissioned by the Council of Trent

---

[1]   Dave Hunt, *A Woman Rides the Beast* (Eugene, Oregon: Harvest House Publishers, 1994) p. 278

to combat the Protestants on theological grounds. They were charged to come up with theological arguments to counter the Protestants' two most damaging doctrinal blows to the mother church: the Protestants' insistence upon justification by faith alone and their identifying of the pope as the Antichrist.

To counter the Protestant and biblical doctrine of justification by faith, the Council of Trent declared that salvation was not a matter of justification alone but also of sanctification. Whereas faith may be sufficient for justification, it was insufficient for sanctification, which, according to the majority vote of the bishops at the Council of Trent, could only be secured through the seven "sacred" sacraments of the Roman Catholic Church—(1) baptism (2) confirmation (3) Eucharist or Mass (4) extreme unction or last rites (5) penance (6) matrimony, and (7) holy orders. With this theological sleight of hand, the Council of Trent condemned all Protestants to hell with more than one hundred anathemas and declared Roman Catholicism to be the only way to heaven.

Although the Council of Trent appears to have easily come up with a heretical equation to counter the Protestant doctrine of justification by faith by simply adding Catholicism's sacraments to faith in Christ as the summation of total salvation, the council's countering of the Protestants' identification of the pope as the Antichrist proved to be a much more difficult challenge. Stepping up to the task for the council was a clever Jesuit priest and doctor of theology by the name of Francisco

Ribera. Ribera postulated that all prophetic Scripture assumed to be alluding to the Antichrist was not applicable in any way to past or present history. Instead, Ribera argued that it all pointed to a time of fulfillment at the end of the age. Consequently, the pope could not be the Antichrist, since the Antichrist would not even appear on the prophetic stage until the playing out of prophecy's final act at the very end of time.

In 1590, Francisco Ribera published his commentary on the book of Revelation. His commentary was intended to provide Catholics with a counter-interpretation of Revelation. Unlike the prevailing Protestant interpretation, which identified the pope as the beast of Revelation, Ribera interpreted the beast as a sinister figure who would appear at the end of time. Far from being the pope, Ribera argued that the beast would be an infidel outside the church who would make an end-time pact with the Jewish people. When it came to the Antichrist being seated in the church, as the Protestant Reformers clearly understood the Apostle Paul to have predicted in 2 Thessalonians 2:3-4, Ribera countered that the "temple" referred to by the apostle in this passage was not the church at all but a rebuilt Jewish temple at the end of time.

Following on the heels of Ribera was another Jesuit scholar, Cardinal Robert Bellarmine. In his "Polemic Lectures Concerning the Disputed Points of the Christian Belief Against the Heretics of this Time," he argued that none of the prophetic Scriptures were applicable in any shape, form, or fashion to the papacy. Furthermore, he condemned all who even hinted at such an interpretation as being guilty of the most loathsome of heresies.

Thanks to Bellarmine, Ribera's new futurist twist on Bible prophecy quickly became the common interpretation among Catholics. This new interpretative view of Bible prophecy eventually became known among Protestants as "Jesuit futurism." Although it has long since lost its previous moniker, being a commonly accepted interpretation of Bible prophecy among both Protestants and Catholics today, the fact that this futurist view originated with the Jesuits during the Counter-Reformation should cause no little angst among all its modern-day Protestant adherents.

All honest researchers are left with a couple of inevitable conclusions—Francisco Ribera is the father of futurism, and this popular modern-day interpretive view of Bible prophecy was spawned by the Catholic Church in defense of its pope against the "beastly" allegations of the Protestant Reformers!

There is certainly much more to the history of the futurist view of Bible prophecy than what we have covered in these few short paragraphs. Still, the simple point we have made in our brief discussion is the salient point vital to our present purpose. Whereas some may desire to color this history in different shades and hues, all honest researchers are left with a couple of inevitable conclusions—Francisco Ribera is the father of futurism, and this popular modern-day interpretive view of Bible prophecy was spawned by the Catholic Church in defense of its pope against the "beastly" allegations of the Protestant Reformers!

Today's most popular school of premillennialism—premillennial dispensationalism—has an even shorter history than the Jesuit futurism from which it sprang. Its history can be traced back no further than the year 1830. It all began with a Scottish lass by the name of Margaret Macdonald.

Margaret Macdonald

In the year 1830, a charismatic revival broke out in western Scotland. In the vicinity of the revival, particularly in Port Glasgow, a small shipbuilding town on the south bank of the river Clyde, there lived a young lady by the name of Margaret Macdonald. Since becoming a Christian a year earlier, Margaret, who was sickly and bedridden, had devoted herself to reading and pondering Scripture.

One day while studying the Scriptures, Margaret claimed to have received an end-time vision. According to her, the vision "burst upon [her] with a glorious light," resulting in "many passages [being] revealed in a light in which [she] had not before seen them."[2] In this new light, a light that none before her had ever possessed, Margaret began interpreting passages of Scripture in ways that no one before her had ever interpreted them.

---

[2] Dave MacPherson, *The Rapture Plot* (Simpsonville, South Carolina: Millennium III Publishers, 1995) p. 250

To begin with, Margaret tied together the "taken" of Matthew 24:40, "Then shall two be in the field; the one shall be taken, and the other left," with the "taken" of 2 Thessalonians 2:7, "For the mystery of iniquity doth already work: only he who now letteth [will let], until he be taken out of the way." By tying these two instances of "taken" together, Margaret became taken with a novel notion; namely, that the Antichrist—"man of sin . . . son of perdition" (2 Thessalonians 2:3)—cannot "be revealed" until Christians are taken out of the world and only the wicked are left behind in it.

Margaret's new slant on the Scripture also led her to couple together Paul's admonition in Ephesians 5:17-18—"Wherefore be ye not unwise, but understanding what the will of the Lord [is]. And be not drunk with wine, wherein is excess; but be filled with the Spirit."—with Christ's parable of the ten virgins in Matthew 25:1-13. By coupling these two passages together, Margaret was able to conclude that the five wise virgins with oil-filled lamps in Christ's parable represent Spirit-filled Christians, while the five foolish and oil-less virgins in the parable represent Christians without the baptism or the filling of the Holy Spirit.

To Margaret Macdonald, the oil needed in the Christian's lamp was the baptism of the Holy Ghost. Any Christian lacking this experience lacked "the light of God," the light by which "we may discern that which cometh not with observation to the natural eye" (Luke 17:20). Thus, all non-charismatic Christians, those unable to "see the sign of [Christ's] appearance," will be left behind with the unbelievers of this world when Christ secretly returns for tongues-speaking, Spirit-filled charismatics alone.

Search if you must, but there is no evidence that anyone in the nineteen centuries of Christian history that preceded Margaret Macdonald ever taught anything like "Maggie's" secret rapture of the church. Although it is a widespread belief in Christendom today, it was unheard of before Margaret Macdonald's day. In addition, in its inception, "Maggie's" novel notion was only a partial rapture of the church, particularly meant for those of her charismatic persuasion. Surely, these facts should at least serve to give pause to all adherents of today's popular secret rapture theory.

> *Search if you must, but there is no evidence that anyone in the nineteen centuries of Christian history that preceded Margaret Macdonald ever taught anything like "Maggie's" secret rapture of the church. Although it is a widespread belief in Christendom today, it was unheard of before Margaret Macdonald's day.*

Understandably, today's evangelical proponents of a secret pretribulation rapture scream bloody murder every time someone traces this popular modern-day doctrine back to its origin. None of its present-day proponents want to give credit where credit is due, to Margaret Macdonald. Furthermore, almost all of them refuse to be associated with Port Glasgow, a town that was not only at the center of the charismatic revival in western Scotland in 1830 but also a hotbed for utterances in tongues on the revival's central theme; namely, Margaret Macdonald's new slant on the second coming of Jesus Christ.

Edward Irving

In the days of Margaret Macdonald, Edward Irving was a renowned Scottish preacher. One could say that he was the Billy Graham of his day, attracting large crowds with his exceptional oratory abilities. Having heard Irving preach on the second coming of Christ near Margaret's home in 1828, Margaret's family began a warm correspondence with the famous pastor of London's Caledonian Chapel at Hatton Garden.

In the spring of 1830, when Margaret received her end-time vision, revealing to her the never-seen-before secret rapture of the church, she sent a handwritten copy of her revelation to Edward Irving as well as to other leading clergymen of the day. Around the same time, reports began to spread of signs and wonders taking place in the Scottish revival. As a result, many traveled to the vicinity of Port Glasgow to check out the supposed phenomena. Among those investigating the revival were members of Irving's Presbyterian church.

Edward Irving was not only in correspondence with the Macdonalds but very much in sympathy with the charismatic revival in western Scotland. As early as 1828, Irving had attributed the conspicuous absence from contemporary churches of the spiritual gifts of the apostolic age to a serious deficiency of faith among the Christians of his day. Thanks to such teaching, tongues and prophetic utterances became so common an occurrence in Irving's church that it became the talk of all London. When the trustees of the church filed a formal complaint over the disruption of their church services by unauthorized utterances, the Presbytery of London was forced into action, removing Irving from his pastorate in 1832. Adding insult to injury, Irving was defrocked in the ensuing year on charges of heresy.

Following his ouster from his Presbyterian church, Irving founded the Catholic Apostolic Church. His leadership of this new church proved short-lived. He died one year later on December 7, 1834. He was only forty-two years old.

Although he is called by some "the father of modern Pentecostalism" and was known in his day for introducing London to the showy, spiritual gifts of Western Scotland's charismatic revival, Edward Irving's greatest legacy is his publicizing of Margaret Macdonald's novel ideas concerning Christ's second coming. After receiving his handwritten copy of Margaret's end-time revelation, Irving's prophetic journal, *The Morning Watch*, published an article in September of 1830 that differentiated between the "epiphany" of Christ, Christ's coming to secretly rapture the church, and the "parousia" of Christ, Christ's coming to judge the world and inaugurate His millennial kingdom.

While subsequent articles appeared in Irving's prophetic journal, some of which expanded upon Margaret Macdonald's initial end-time notions, this September 1830 article appears to be the first time that the secret rapture of the church was taught publicly and in print. What began with the vision of a young Scottish lassie was first publicized and printed by a soon-to-be defrocked Presbyterian minister. Following the defrocked minister's untimely death, the torch of this new doctrine was carried by his followers, who became known as "Irvingites."

John Nelson Darby

Another prominent minister in the days of Margaret Macdonald was John Nelson Darby. Darby started out in the ministry as an ordained Anglican priest but became famous for helping to launch the Plymouth Brethren movement from informal worship services conducted in homes.

Besides being instrumental in the founding of the Plymouth Brethren, Darby is also known as "the father of dispensationalism," a school of biblical interpretation that insists upon Scripture being literally interpreted as well as rightly divided so as to limit the application of each passage to the particular age or dispensation to which it speaks.

An example of Darby's dispensationalism is the Israel/church dichotomy. According to Darby, nothing God ever said to Israel should be applied to the church, and nothing God ever said to the church should be applied to Israel. God's plans for Israel and the church are totally different and must be kept separate from one another at all times. In addition, these separate plans can never operate concurrently upon the earth, since God only works in one dispensation at a time. Thus, if God is to ever turn back to His plan for Israel, He must first take the church out of the world, bringing to an end this current dispensation—the church age. Only then can God fulfill His literal promises to the physical descendants of Abraham. Of course, this teaching necessitates a belief in a secret rapture of the church prior to the premillennial dispensationalist's supposed seven-year tribulation period.

Although there is no evidence of it in his writing or preaching before 1831, Darby claimed to have formulated his new view of biblical interpretation during a lengthy convalescence that followed his being thrown by a horse in 1827. Still, it wasn't after being thrown by a horse but after visiting Glasgow during the charismatic revival of 1830 that Darby began preaching and teaching premillennial dispensationalism.

That Darby visited Glasgow at the height of the charismatic revival and heard nothing about Margaret Macdonald's end-time revelation, which by then had become the central theme of the revival's tongues and prophetic utterances, is inconceivable. Equally

Darby may be the "father of dispensationalism," but Margaret Macdonald, Edward Irving, and the "Irvingites" were already serving up a secret rapture of the church before Darby ever sat down at the table.

inconceivable is any suggestion that Darby was ignorant of Edward Irving's taking of Margaret's end-time revelation to the pulpit and to the press. Darby may be the "father of dispensationalism," but Margaret Macdonald, Edward Irving, and the "Irvingites" were already serving up a secret rapture of the church before Darby ever sat down at the table.

Today's premillennial dispensationalists proudly trace their eschatology back to the orthodox and biblically sound John Nelson Darby. They refuse, however, to have their end-time views associated with a young Scottish lassie, a defrocked Presbyterian pastor, and the defrocked minister's heretical followers. Yet, the truth is, all of these were running with the premillennial dispensationalists' pet doctrine—the secret rapture of the church—before the premillennial dispensationalists' alleged progenitor ever got out of the starting blocks.

While he cannot be credited as the originator of the doctrine of premillennial dispensationalism's secret rapture, John Nelson Darby can and should be credited with birthing, systematizing, and proliferating premillennial dispensationalism. He and his Plymouth Brethren were preaching it in Ireland as early as 1831 and soon thereafter propagating it to other parts of the world.

Cyrus Ingerson Scofield

John Nelson Darby visited the United States at least five times. Although he won few converts to his new views of biblical interpretation and eschatology, he was able to win over some influential American evangelicals. One of these, John Inglis, used his magazine, *Waymarks in the Wilderness*, to introduce premillennial dispensationalism to North America. Another, James H. Brookes, pastor of Walnut Street Presbyterian Church in St. Louis, Missouri, organized the Niagara Bible Conference for the express purpose of disseminating premillennial dispensationalism in this country.

One of the Reverend James Brookes's parishioners, who also attended the Niagara Bible Conference, was a lawyer by the name of Cyrus Ingerson Scofield. C. I. Scofield became so enamored with premillennial dispensationalism that he devoted himself to the publishing of an annotated study Bible containing his own study notes on premillennial dispensationalism. Published in 1909, Scofield's study Bible proved to be a literary coup for premillennial dispensationalists. Nothing in the history of this country has ever done more to legitimize premillennial dispensationalism than the Scofield Reference Bible.

> Nothing in the history of this country has ever done more to legitimize premillennial dispensationalism than the Scofield Reference Bible.

Hal Lindsey

Whereas the Scofield Reference Bible may be credited for doing more than anything else to legitimize premillennial dispensationalism in the United States, it was Hal Lindsey's 1970 bestseller, *The Late Great Planet Earth*, that did more than anything else to popularize premillennial dispensationalism in this country. Lindsey's book not only sold millions of copies but was also adapted into a motion picture narrated by Orson Wells in 1979. Unlike previous books on prophecy, which were sold only in Christian bookstores, Lindsey's book was sold in secular bookstores right alongside gothic romances, cheap westerns, and books on dieting, organic gardening, and UFOs. It could even be picked up along with the latest celebrity scandal sheet in the checkout line of your

It was Hal Lindsey's 1970 bestseller, The Late Great Planet Earth, that did more than anything else to popularize premillennial dispensationalism in this country.

local drugstore or supermarket. As a result, Lindsey's book exposed a far wider audience to premillennial dispensationalism. It wasn't just Christian prophecy wonks who bought and read Lindsey's book and paid to see the movie adaptation but scores of unbelievers as well, people who had no previous knowledge of nor interest in Bible prophecy.

Tim LaHaye

Much like Hal Lindsey's *The Late Great Planet Earth*, Tim LaHaye and Jerry Jenkins's series of *Left Behind* novels have exposed millions of people to premillennial dispensationalism. Incredibly, over 40 million copies in the series have been sold to date. In 2000, the first novel in the series was made into a full-length motion picture, *Left Behind: The Movie*. However, due to the movie's dismal performance at the box office, two subsequent sequels have been released straight to video and DVD, *Left Behind II: Tribulation Force* and *Left Behind: World at War.* Truly, LaHaye and Jenkins's books have done what Lindsey's book did before them: they have publicized and leant credence to the beliefs of premillennial dispensationalism.

Conclusion

These brief histories of modern-day schools of eschatology neither prove nor disprove the beliefs of their respective proponents. Granted, they may cause no little angst among their adherents, heighten suspicions among their skeptics, or even lend some credence to the few with a component or two traceable back to the first century. Still, one should not reject, receive, nor retain a particular view of eschatology on the basis of its history; one should do so only on the basis of its Scriptural soundness. With this said, let us all agree that there is no room in the study of biblical eschatology for dogmatism or the denunciation of others with differing views, but there is plenty of room for further debate and honest discussion among all true Bible believers who both love and look for Christ's appearing (2 Timothy 4:8).

5

Interpreting Bible Prophecy

There is probably no other issue that will prove to be more determinative in your understanding of Bible prophecy than whether you interpret it literally or figuratively. Some within the church today insist upon a literal interpretation of the prophetic Scriptures. They tend to look down their noses at all who disagree with them. They even accuse those of interpreting the prophetic Scriptures allegorically of being heretics who deny the plain truth of God's Word.

On the other hand, there are others within the church today who insist upon a figurative interpretation of the prophetic Scriptures. They tend to look down their noses at everyone who disagrees with them. They accuse everyone who favors a literal interpretation of the prophetic Scriptures of being simpletons who incessantly misinterpret the Word of God because of their silly simplemindedness.

If we could rise above the fray, however, and take an honest look at both interpretive camps—the literal and the figurative—we would discover that no one in the literal camp always interprets the prophetic Scriptures literally, nor does anyone in the figurative camp always interpret the prophetic Scriptures figuratively. There are times when common sense dictates to those within the literal camp that something in the prophetic Scriptures must be interpreted figuratively, just as there are times when common sense dictates to those within the figurative camp that something in the prophetic Scriptures must be interpreted literally.

There are obviously things in the Bible that are to be understood literally. Take for example the seventh commandment: Thou shalt not commit adultery (Exodus 20:14). There's nothing figurative about this commandment. It's plain and simple. The Bible says "thou shalt not" and we shouldn't; case closed. Yet, there are other things in the Bible that are obviously meant to be understood figuratively. For instance, Jesus once said, "And if your right eye offends you, pluck it out, and cast it from you" (Matthew 5:29). It doesn't require a high spiritual IQ to figure out that this verse is to be understood figuratively, not literally. Our Lord is obviously not advocating that we literally pluck out our eyes and throw them away.

Sometimes all it takes to determine if something in the Bible should be interpreted literally or figuratively is a little common sense. We use common sense every day of our lives to make these kinds of determinations about things we hear or read. We hear about some lady getting horribly upset and "having a cow."

We hear someone speak of a torrential downpour as "raining cats and dogs" or a friend tells us that he got a speeding ticket for "flying down the road in his car." Common sense dictates to us that we interpret all of these metaphors figuratively rather than literally; after all, we know that women don't have cows, it doesn't rain cats and dogs, and automobiles can't fly.

There are occasions, however, when common sense alone will not provide us with all that we need to determine whether we should interpret something in the prophetic Scriptures literally or figuratively. On these occasions, we must be careful not to fall into one of two common errors. The first error is to interpret the Scripture too figuratively; that is, to read too much into it. Many people are guilty of reading things into the Scripture that aren't there. The second error is to interpret the Scripture too literally; that is, to see only the literal surface of the Scripture and to fail to see its deeper spiritual truths. While many today are always warning us about the dangers of over-spiritualizing the Scripture, I fear that the far greater danger today is to overlook the Scripture's spiritual meaning because of our current equating of literalism with orthodoxy.

As any good Bible student knows, there are some basic rules of hermeneutics—the proper method or theory by which one should interpret the Bible. To begin with, each passage must be studied within its immediate context. No passage can be properly interpreted or implemented if taken out of its context. It has been said, and rightfully so, as proven by many a modern-day cult, that you can twist the Scriptures into saying anything. For instance, the Bible says in one place that Judas went out and hanged himself; then, in another place, the Bible says, "Go do thou likewise."

Along with interpreting each passage in its immediate context, one should also give careful consideration to each passage's historical background and grammatical peculiarities. This calls for special attention to be paid to such things as verb tenses, literary type, and figures of speech.

Another important rule of hermeneutics is to always compare Scripture with Scripture. All Scripture should be interpreted in the light of all other Scripture. The Bible will not contradict in one place what it says in another. Any perceived contradictions are in our minds, never on the pages of Holy Writ. The serious student of Scripture should always remember that the best commentary on the Bible is the Bible!

Among the basic rules of hermeneutics is what has been referred to as the Golden Rule of Biblical Interpretation. According to this Golden Rule, when the plain sense of Scripture makes common sense, we should seek no other sense. In other words, unless the commentary of other related Scriptures or the immediate context of the passage under consideration indicate otherwise, we should always take every word at its primary, ordinary, usual, and literal meaning.

I personally like this paraphrased version of the Golden Rule of Biblical Interpretation: when the plain sense of Scripture makes common sense, we should seek no other sense, lest we be led into nonsense. Permit me to illustrate what is meant by "nonsense."

Why Fire Engines Are Red

Fire engines are red because they have eight wheels and four people ride them. Eight and four is twelve. Twelve is a foot. A foot is a ruler. Queen Elizabeth was a ruler. Queen Elizabeth was the name of a ship that sailed on the sea. Fish swim in the sea. Fish have fins. The Finns fought the Russians. The Russians are red. Fire engines are always rushin', so fire engines are always red.

Obviously, the above is nothing more than a bunch of nonsense. It has absolutely nothing to do with why fire engines are red.

If we're not careful, we can be guilty of twisting the sacred Scriptures into nonsense with our imaginative interpretations. Whether it's the espousing of some secret "Bible code" deciphered by the calculations of computer geeks or some esoteric meaning revealed by a supposed divine epiphany to some self-proclaimed present-day seer, there is no shortage of people today attempting to impose their nonsense on the plain sense of Scripture. While we, the lone stewards of the Scripture, must guard the sacred text against such debasement at the hands of others, we must also see to it that we are never guilty of handling the Scripture in some willy-nilly fashion.

We simply must not take liberties with the Scriptures by interpreting them too figuratively. We should never read too much into them, making something of them that we shouldn't or stretching them further than God ever intended. Though much of the Scripture must be interpreted figuratively in order to be properly understood, we must not employ elastic exegesis so as to make the Scripture pliable enough to encompass every figurative figment of a hyperactive imagination.

As important as it is to steer ourselves clear of interpreting the Scriptures too figuratively, the far greater danger today is that of interpreting the Scriptures too literally. As I've already remarked, literalism is commonly equated with orthodoxy in many a contemporary Christian circle. Therefore, many Christians today exclusively interpret the Scriptures literally, for fear of being accused of apostasy over some allegorical understanding of the Bible's apocalyptic literature. However, much of the Bible's apocalyptic literature is hyperbolic and figurative, making its literal interpretation both inadequate and inaccurate.

To have any chance at interpreting the Bible correctly, especially at interpreting the prophetic Scriptures correctly, I believe that there are three vital truths that every Christian must know.

1. The Whole Bible Is About Jesus

To the religious leaders of His day, our Lord once said, "Search the Scriptures; for in them you think you have eternal life: and they are they which testify of me. And you will not come to me, that you might have life" (John 5:39-40). According to Jesus, He is the subject of Scripture. He is what the Bible is all about. The Scriptures were written to "testify" of Him. This explains why the Baptist Faith & Message—our Southern Baptist confession of faith—boldly declares: "All Scripture is a testimony to Christ, who is Himself the focus of divine revelation."

No matter what or where you are reading in the Bible, it is in some way or another telling you something, teaching you something, or showing you something about Jesus Christ. For this reason, our ministry's—Time For Truth Ministries'—confession of faith contains the following statement on the Scriptures: "We believe that the Bible is the divinely inspired, inerrant, and infallible Word of God. It has Christ for its subject, salvation for its end, and truth, without error for its content. It is therefore the sole authority for faith and practice."

The prophetic Scriptures are no different from the rest of the Scriptures. They, too, are all about Jesus. For instance, consider the first words of the first verse of the first chapter of the Bible's most famous prophetic book: "The Revelation of Jesus Christ" (Revelation 1:1). Many people believe that Revelation is a book about the revelation of the future; however, the book plainly states in its opening salvo that it is about the revelation of Jesus Christ.

The purpose of the book of Revelation is the same as the purpose of all of the other books of the Bible; it is to reveal Jesus Christ to us. In fact, the purpose of the whole Bible—the written Word of God—is to get us to Christ, the living Word of God. If the Bible can't do this for us, it really can't help us, since it's Jesus alone who can save us.

> The purpose of the whole Bible—the written Word of God—is to get us to Christ, the living Word of God.

In Luke 24:44-45, the resurrected Christ attempts to help His disciples over the hurdle of doubt by "opening their understanding" to "the Scriptures." Christ does this by walking them through the Scripture and showing them everything "in the law of Moses, and in the prophets, and in the psalms, concerning [Him]." Like Christ's disciples, we will never arrest our doubts or truly understand God's Word until we, too, are seeing Jesus in "the law of Moses, and in the prophets, and in the psalms." In other words, we'll never understand the Bible until we're seeing Jesus in every verse on every page.

> We'll never understand the Bible until we're seeing Jesus in every verse on every page.

Of course, all of this translates into the fact that much of the Bible, especially types-of-Christ with which the pages of Scripture are riddled, must be interpreted both literally and figuratively. It's really not a matter of either-or, but of both-and. Permit me to demonstrate the recurring demand for dual interpretations in order to rightly divide the Word of Truth (2 Timothy 2:15).

Was there a literal King of Salem named Melchizedek? Yes, and you may read about him in Genesis 14:18-20. Yet, according to Hebrews 7:1-28, his appearance in Scripture is to be understood figuratively. He was a type-of-Christ, typifying Christ as our eternal High Priest.

Was there a literal Passover lamb sacrificed by the children of Israel in Egypt? Yes, and you may read about it in Exodus 12:1-51. Yet, according to the Apostle Paul, its appearance in Scripture is to be understood figuratively (1 Corinthians 5:7). It was a type-of-Christ, typifying Him as "our passover [who was] sacrificed for us" so that the judgment of God will pass over all who believe in Him—the consummate paschal Lamb.

Was there a literal rock from which Israel received life-saving water in the wilderness? Yes, and you may read about it in Exodus 17:1-7. Yet, according to the Apostle Paul, its appearance in Scripture is to be understood figuratively (1 Corinthians 10:4). It, too, was a type-of-Christ, typifying Christ as our life-saving spiritual sustenance in the wilderness of this fallen world.

Was there a literal tabernacle in the wilderness and later temple in Jerusalem? Yes, and you may read about them in several places in the Scripture. Yet, the Scripture also teaches in several places that both the tabernacle and the temple are to be understood figuratively. They both serve as types-of Christ, typifying His miraculous and multifaceted ministry.

In all of these examples, there is a literal surface to the Scripture, but beneath the literal surface lies the Scripture's deeper spiritual meaning. To fail to figuratively mine beneath the Scripture's literal surface is not only to rob ourselves of the Bible's most precious gems of truth but also to greatly impoverish ourselves spiritually.

To fail to figuratively mine beneath the Scripture's literal surface is not only to rob ourselves of the Bible's most precious gems of truth but also to greatly impoverish ourselves spiritually.

2. The Old Testament Contains Physical Illustrations of the Spiritual Truths Taught in the New Testament

In a remarkable passage of Scripture, 1 Corinthians 10:1-13, the Apostle Paul teaches us that Old Testament stories, such as Israel's miraculous crossing of the Red Sea, guidance in the wilderness by a cloud, eating of life-sustaining manna from heaven, and drinking of life-saving water from a rock, are all recorded as "examples" for us, "upon whom the ends of the world are come." In other words, the Old Testament is comprised of physical types and shadows that serve as illustrations of the spiritual truths we are taught in the New Testament.

It is often said, and rightly so, that the Old Testament is the New Testament concealed, and the New Testament is the Old Testament revealed. Herein lies the importance of studying the Old Testament in these New Testament times. Even though we are no longer under the old covenant, the study of its types and shadows sheds invaluable light upon the realities and substance of the new covenant. Indeed, without a proper understanding of the Old Testament, no one can possibly understand the New Testament.

Let's pinpoint an Old Testament example of a New Testament truth. In His famous Sermon on the Mount, our Lord teaches the following profound truth: "But seek you first the kingdom of God, and his righteousness; and all these things shall be added unto you" (Matthew 6:33). Although there are many Old Testament examples of this New Testament truth, we will limit our consideration to one: King Solomon's request for wisdom (1 Kings 3:5-15).

After being crowned his father David's successor, Solomon had a dream in which the Lord appeared unto him. In the dream, God promised to grant Solomon a wish. Solomon could have wished for anything he wanted. He could have wished for long life, for victory over his enemies, or for fabulous wealth. Instead, he wished for wisdom. First and foremost, Solomon wanted to please God by wisely governing God's people.

As a result of putting God first, Solomon not only received what he wished for but also what he didn't wish for—long life, victory over his enemies, and fabulous wealth. Here, in this Old Testament story, is a physical picture that unveils for us a profound truth that was taught by our Savior in His most famous New Testament sermon. Undoubtedly, this highlights the value of Old Testament study in these New Testament times.

While it is essential for us to learn from the Old Testament, it is a grave error to live in it. In Colossians 2:16-17, the Apostle Paul admonishes us not to live in the shadows of the Old Testament (that is, in the Old Testament's types-of-Christ) but in the substance of the New Testament (that is, in Jesus Christ Himself). For instance, why should we still observe the shadow of the Jewish Sabbath when the substance of it can now be enjoyed daily by every Christian who is at rest in Christ (Hebrews 4:1-11)?

Just as Paul instructs us to shrug-off the condemnation of others over our failure to observe "Sabbath days," we should also spurn any contemporary eschatology that is vague on New Testament substance and fraught with Old Testament shadows. Too much of today's interpretation of the prophetic Scriptures is based upon a literal reading of Old Testament types and shadows rather than upon a figurative interpretation

We should spurn any contemporary eschatology that is vague on New Testament substance and fraught with Old Testament shadows.

that points us to what they actually symbolize—namely, present-day spiritual realities. As a result, many contemporary Christians have bought into a spiritual "back to the future," believing that the ultimate fulfillment of Bible prophecy will be a return to Old Testament types and shadows, such as the reestablishment of national Israel, a rebuilt Jewish temple, a re-instituted Levitical priesthood, and the restarting of animal sacrifices.

3. The Book of Revelation Is a Book of Signs and Symbols

In the very first verse of the very first chapter of the book of Revelation, we are told that the Bible's most famous prophetic book was "signified" by an angel to Christ's servant John. To signify something means to communicate it in signs and symbols. The book of Revelation is therefore a book of signs and symbols.

As a self-proclaimed book of signs and symbols, the book of Revelation necessitates a figurative rather than a literal interpretation. Now, this is not to say that nothing in the book is to be taken literally, but that the book itself can only be properly interpreted figuratively. In this book, candles aren't necessarily candles, stars aren't necessarily stars, beasts aren't necessarily beasts, and cities aren't necessarily cities. Instead, these things are symbolic of other things. Thus, to properly understand the book of Revelation, one must first understand what its signs and symbols symbolize.

It is here, specifically, at the insistence that prophetic symbolism must be understood symbolically, that many in the contemporary church cry, "Foul!" According to them, anything other than a literal interpretation of Scripture runs afoul of Christian orthodoxy. They not only propose that a figurative interpretation of the prophetic Scriptures leads to a misrepresentation of the sacred text but also to a downright denial of scriptural truths.

Out of fear of being branded by today's literalists as a heretic, many a contemporary Christian has sunk down into the fictional world of Tim LaHaye and Jerry Jenkins. Yet, such a literal interpretation of the prophetic Scriptures, especially the book of Revelation—a book of signs and symbols—invariably leads to a misunderstanding of all portions of divine revelation that necessitate a figurative interpretation. This is particularly true of the prophetic Scriptures and the Bible's hyperbolic apocalyptic literature.

Did you know that Jesus Christ did not literally interpret all prophetic Scriptures? In Malachi 4:5, Malachi, the last of the Old Testament prophets, predicted that "Elijah the prophet" would come before "the great and dreadful day of the Lord." According to Jesus, this prophecy was figuratively, not literally, fulfilled in John the Baptist (Matthew 11:13-14; 17:10-13). Obviously, Elijah did not literally come in the person of John the Baptist, but the Baptist figuratively fulfilled this prophecy by being so much like Elijah—by coming "in the spirit and power of Elijah" and by having a ministry like Elijah's; that is, he had a ministry of turning the people back to God in preparation for the promised coming Messiah (Luke 1:15-17).

Like our Lord, the Apostle Peter also understood the figurative aspect of the Bible's apocalyptic literature. He boldly proclaimed on the day of Pentecost that the coming of the Holy Spirit was in fulfillment of the prophecy of the ancient prophet Joel (Acts 2:14-21; Joel 2:28-32). It is easy to see in the birth of the church and the commencement of the church's gospel preaching, the Pentecostal fulfillment of Joel's predicted outpouring of the Holy Spirit and obtainable salvation for "whosoever shall call upon the name of the Lord." What is not so readily apparent, however, is the Pentecostal fulfillment of Joel's predicted "wonders in heaven" and "signs in the earth."

How did Pentecost fulfill Joel's prediction of "blood, and fire, and vapor of smoke: The sun [being] turned into darkness, and the moon into blood"? Since we know from the preaching of Peter that Joel's prophecy was fulfilled at Pentecost, despite the fact that these elements of it were not literally fulfilled, we are forced to either look for a figurative fulfillment of these elements of the prophecy or to admit a biblical contradiction. Confident that the latter is impossible, we turn to the former for an answer to our quandary.

Pentecost was, among other things, a commemoration of God's giving of the Law to Israel. It commemorated God's coming down in the midst of His people in power at Mount Sinai. This historic event in the history of Israel was accompanied by "signs" and "wonders" commensurate with those contained in Joel's prophecy (Exodus 19:10-25). The sight of it all was so frightening that even Moses was terrified and trembled with fear (Hebrews 12:21).

Although not accompanied by such literal and terrifying signs and wonders as warnings to all of the inaccessibility of a Holy God, Pentecost served as a fulfillment of Joel's prophecy and the substantive realization of all that Sinai symbolized and Pentecost commemorated. God once again came down in the midst of His people in power. This time, however, it wasn't on Mount Sinai to give birth to His Old Testament people, Israel, but on Mount Zion (Jerusalem) to give birth to His New Testament people, the church (Hebrews 12:18-24). Instead of coming down in "fire and smoke" to give His Law, which was written on stone tablets, God came down at Pentecost in "cloven tongues like as of fire" to give His Spirit, so that His Law could henceforth be written on the "fleshly tablets of human hearts" (Jeremiah 31:31-33; 2 Corinthians 3:3).

Unlike the accompanying signs at Sinai, which served as warnings to one and all of the inaccessibility of God, the accompanying signs at Pentecost, such as every man hearing the gospel in his own language, served as proof of the accessibility of God to all who place their faith in Jesus Christ. Whereas Sinai served as the giving of the letter of the Law, resulting in the death of three thousand, Pentecost served as the giving of the Spirit of the Law, resulting in the salvation of three thousand (2 Corinthians 3:6; Exodus 32:28; Acts 2:41).

In spite of Peter's plain proclamation of its Pentecostal fulfillment, Joel's prophecy is still seen as awaiting some further and future fulfillment by today's literalists, who insist upon literal blood, fire, vapor of smoke, a darkened sun, and a bloody moon. It is this kind of biblical interpretation that gets smoke in our eyes and keeps us from seeing the true spiritual meaning of many a biblical prophecy. By losing ourselves in the search for literal smoke, we end up missing the profound spiritual significance of both Joel's prophecy and the day of Pentecost.

Like our Lord and the Apostle Peter, James, the leader of the church in Jerusalem, also interpreted some biblical prophecies figuratively. In the first church council, the Council at Jerusalem, James interprets the prophet Amos' prediction of the restoration of the tabernacle of David as being fulfilled by the Gentiles' acceptance of the gospel of Jesus Christ (Amos 9:11-12; Acts 15:13-18). According to James, the salvation of the Gentiles was the predicted rebuilding of David's fallen tent.

The tabernacle of David, unlike the temple in Jerusalem, had no separating courts and dividing walls. It was open for all men to approach God. Thus, James interpreted Amos' prophecy as being figuratively fulfilled by the fact that the gospel makes it possible for all people, Jews and Gentiles, to once again come to God. The prophecy of Amos was not literally fulfilled by the putting up of a tent to house temple furniture and furnishings, but it was figuratively fulfilled by the gospel's "whosoever will may come."

When Christ came the first time, the people of God missed out on "the time of their visitation" (Luke 19:44). This was due in no small part to Israel's insistence upon a literal interpretation of Bible prophecy. The Jews were expecting a military king riding on a charger, so they overlooked a meek King who rode into Jerusalem on a colt. They expected their Messiah to save them from Rome, so they overlooked Him who came to save them from sin. They were looking for an earthly kingdom, so they overlooked Him who came to establish a heavenly kingdom. As a result of a strict literal interpretation of the prophetic Scriptures and a refusal to "spiritualize" anything that the prophets had predicted, the people of Israel, who looked for a Messiah to deliver them from Rome, ended up rejecting their Messiah and being destroyed by Rome.

Even our Lord's disciples were still questioning Him about an earthly kingdom for Israel just prior to His ascension (Acts 1:6). Interestingly, He had just instructed them to go to Jerusalem and wait until they received "the promise of the Father," which He described to them as an impending baptism with the Holy Spirit (Acts 1:4-5). However, this stupendous promise of the pouring out of the Spirit on the day of Pentecost was like water on a duck's back to Jewish disciples who were obsessed with an earthly kingdom for Israel.

Our Lord responded to His disciples' question by instructing them to leave such matters in the hands of the Almighty (Acts 1:7). He then attempted to divert their attention from an earthly and exclusive kingdom for Jews to a heavenly and inclusive kingdom for all people. He did so by explaining to them that they were about to be empowered by the Holy Spirit to take His message not just to "Jerusalem and all Judea," but also to "Samaria and unto the uttermost part of the earth" (Acts 1:8).

In Mark 9:1, Jesus promised His contemporaries that some of them would "not taste death, till they [saw] the kingdom of God come with power." When was this promise of our Lord fulfilled? Obviously, it was on Pentecost, when the Holy Spirit was given to empower Christ's witnesses to advance God's kingdom by the preaching of a worldwide gospel. Yet, just prior to this most momentous event, Christ's disciples were still focused on a coming kingdom for their own people rather than on a kingdom coming with God's power.

According to Jesus, His "kingdom is not of this world" (John 18:36). Furthermore, it has already come, as proven by his miraculous works, such as casting out devils "with the finger of God" (Luke 11:20). Contrary to the thinking of many, Jesus taught that "the kingdom of God doesn't come with observation" (Luke 17:20-21). You can't say, "here it is" or "there it is," for "the kingdom of God is within you." It is found in the hearts of those who have voluntarily submitted themselves to the rule and reign of Christ.

Scripture teaches that the kingdom of God has come, is here, and is coming. It commenced at Christ's first coming, coming with the power of the Holy Spirit on the day of Pentecost; it continues today in the hearts of believers, who are Christ's Spirit-empowered witnesses and willing subjects; and it will be consummated at Christ's second coming, when all things shall be summed up in Him who shall reign forever and ever!

As we approach the second coming of Jesus Christ, I'm afraid that the people of God today are once again failing to understand the prophetic Scriptures due to our insistence upon a literal interpretation of them all. For instance, consider the following:

- In today's church, we're all hung up on a rebuilt temple in Jerusalem, instead of upon the church, which is "the temple of God" and "the new Jerusalem" (Ephesians 2:21-22; Revelation 21:1-27).

- In today's church, we're all hung up on "Mount Sinai," the reinstitution of the Levitical priesthood and animal sacrifices, instead of upon "Mount Zion," "the heavenly Jerusalem" and "city of the living God," within which all men are priests, having been cleansed from their sin by "the sprinkled blood" of their High Priest and "Mediator" Jesus Christ (Hebrews 12:18-24).

- In today's church, we're all hung up on natural Jews who are outwardly circumcised in the flesh and children of Abraham because of their physical birth, instead of upon supernatural Jews who are inwardly circumcised in the heart, transformed into a new creation in Christ, and children of God because of their spiritual birth (Romans 2:28-29; Galatians 6:12-16).

- In today's church, we're all hung up on the nation of Israel and its Jewish exclusiveness, instead of upon spiritual Israel and its universal inclusiveness (Romans 2:28-29; 10:12; Galatians 3:26-29; 6:16).

- In today's church, we're all hung up on Old Testament types and shadows, instead of upon New Testament substance and realities.

It was the Apostle Paul who wrote, "We look not at the things which are seen, but at the things which are not seen: for the things which are seen are temporal; but the things which are not seen are eternal" (2 Corinthians 4:18). Truly, today's church needs to get its attention off the visible, physical, and temporal, and get its attention on the invisible, spiritual, and eternal. If we fail to do so, we're going to miss out on what's going on in these last of the last days.

Permit me to conclude with a current and clear example of the danger of interpreting the prophetic Scriptures too literally. There are only three monotheistic faiths—faiths that believe in only one God—in all the world today. The oldest of the three is Judaism; the next is Christianity; and the youngest of the three is Islam.

All three of our world's monotheistic faiths trace themselves back to the same man, Abraham. Judaism traces itself back to Abraham through Isaac, Abraham's son by his wife Sarah. Islam traces itself back to Abraham through Ishmael, Abraham's son by his wife's handmaid Hagar. And Christianity traces itself back to Abraham through the "promised seed of Abraham," Jesus Christ (Galatians 3:16, 26-29).

Judaism is a Jewish religion. It distinguishes between Jews and Gentiles, elevating Jews alone as the chosen people of God. Although Gentiles can become Jewish proselytes, they can never become Jews. Consequently, all Gentile adherents to Judaism are allotted second-class status, since they are merely proselytes to the Jewish faith and not the true progeny of Abraham.

Islam is an Arab religion, despite the fact that most of today's Muslims are not Arabs. Islam's founder, the prophet Mohammed, taught that Arabs were superior to all other people. According to Mohammed, Arabs should be loved for three reasons: first, because Mohammed himself was an Arab; second, because the Koran is written in Arabic; and finally, because the only language spoken in paradise is Arabic.

Unlike the other two monotheistic faiths, Christianity is a universal faith. Our God is "no respecter of persons" (Acts 10:34). "Whosoever will may come" to Christ, and when we come to Christ, there is "no difference" between us in Christ (John 3:16; Revelation 22:17; Romans 10:12-13; Colossians 3:11). It doesn't matter if you are an Arab or a Jew. It doesn't matter if you are a Jew or a Gentile. It doesn't matter if you are red or yellow, black or white. All that matters is that you believe in Jesus, and all who believe in Jesus become one in Him. We're all equal; the ground at the cross is level.

For centuries, Arabs and Jews have been fighting over Middle-Eastern real estate. As natural descendants of Abraham—the Jews through Isaac and the Arabs through Ishmael—both claim rightful ownership of the land God promised to Abraham. The refusal of either side to relinquish their claim to the Promised Land is deeply rooted in their respective religions. Thus, the Middle-East has always been and will continue to be the hotspot of our world and the world's foremost flashpoint.

Unlike the Jews and Arabs, who are the physical descendants of Abraham, Christians, who are the only true spiritual descendants of Abraham, should not be hung up on Middle-Eastern real estate. Instead, we should be looking for what Abraham looked for himself. What was it that Abraham, who the New Testament identifies as "the father of all who believe," both Jews and Gentiles, was really after? According to the famous faith chapter of the Bible, it wasn't Middle-Eastern real estate, but "a better country, that is, [a] heavenly [one] ... whose builder and maker is God" (Hebrews 11:10, 16).

Abraham wasn't concerned about a promised plot of dirt in the Middle East; he was concerned about what it symbolized and represented, a promised place prepared for him by Christ in the Father's house (John 14:1-3). Rather than being all enthralled over whether Jews or Gentiles control Middle-Eastern real estate, what we ought to be enthralled over is whether or not Jews and Gentiles are going to heaven. It's time that today's church got its feet off terra firma and it's head in the clouds—that is to say, it's time we stopped concentrating on the literal earthly patterns and shadows of heavenly things and started concentrating on what they symbolize; namely, it's time that we focused on the heavenly things themselves (Colossians 2:17; Hebrews 8:5; 9:23-24; 10:1). Only then will we be able to rightly interpret for our times and implement in our lives the truths of the prophetic Scriptures.

> Rather than being all enthralled over whether Jews or Gentiles control Middle-Eastern real estate, what we ought to be enthralled over is whether or not Jews and Gentiles are going to heaven.

The second volume of this series—Piecing Together Bible Prophecy—*is soon to be released. It is entitled:* The Most Amazing Prophecy in the Bible. *Subsequent volumes will follow.*

Don Walton is the founder and director of Time For Truth Ministries. He is also a pastor, revivalist, conference speaker, and author of several books and booklets. You may email Don at don@timefortruth.org.